The eyes of the court are on Marie Antoinette.
Times change, and even the most fashionable
queens go out of style. Drawing comparison of
the gluttonous excess of Marie's era to the decadent material-
ism of the present day, _Marie Antoinette_ holds up a mirror to
our contemporary society, which just might be entertaining
itself to death.

DAVID ADJMI is the recipient of a Guggenheim Fellowship, the Whiting Writers' Award, the Kesselring Fellowship, a Steinberg Playwright Award (the "Mimi"), and the
Bush Artist Fellowship. His as-yet-untitled memoir is forth-
coming from HarperCollins. David is a graduate of Sarah
Lawrence College, the Iowa Playwrights Workshop, and the
Juilliard School.

Marie Antoinette

---⟋∞⟍---

(1789)

# Marie Antoinette

(1789)

DAVID ADJMI

THEATRE COMMUNICATIONS GROUP
NEW YORK
2017

*Marie Antoinette* is published by Theatre Communications Group, Inc., 520 Eighth Avenue, 24th Floor, New York, NY 10018-4156

French translation on pages 85–86 courtesy of Marissa Skudlarek.

The publication of *Marie Antoinette* by David Adjmi, through TCG's Book Program, is made possible in part by the New York State Council on the Arts with the support of Governor Andrew Cuomo and the New York State Legislature.

TCG books are exclusively distributed to the book trade by Consortium Book Sales and Distribution.

Library of Congress Control Numbers:
2015049371 (print) / 2016001978 (ebook)
ISBN 978-1-55936-494-2 (softcover) / ISBN 978-1-55936-805-6 (ebook)
A catalog record for this book is available from the Library of Congress.

Book design and composition by Lisa Govan
Cover illustrations by Bee Murphy

First Edition, October 2017

## Thank You

Aaron Stone; Adam Greenfield and Playwrights Horizons; Daniel Talbott and Addie Johnson Talbott; Anna Chlumsky; Maria Dizzia; Bill Buell; Brooke Bloom; Catherine Sheehy; Colleen Werthmann; Darren Goldstein; David Greenspan; Deney Terrio; Diane Borger, Diane Paulus and everyone at American Repertory Theater; Dramatists Guild Fund; Eddie Cahill; Fran Offenhauser and Michael Mekeel; Gabrielle Calvocoressi and Angeline Shaka; Gary Wilmes; Gloria Peterson and James McCarthy; Greg Keller; Hannah Cabell; Heidi Schreck; Howard Sherman; Jackson Gay; Jake Silbermann; James Bundy, Victoria Nolan, Jennifer Kiger, Steven Padla and all my friends at Yale Repertory Theatre; Jenny Schwartz; Jo Lampert; Josh Hamilton; Judith Ivey; Karole Armitage; Kate Buddeke; Kathleen Tolan; Kirsten Greenidge; Laura Esterman; Maria Striar and Clubbed Thumb; Marin Ireland; Mark Subias, Emma Feiwel, Rachel Viola and everyone at United Talent Agency; Matt Wolf; Mindy Walder; Morgan Jenness; Emily Morse, Todd London and everyone at New Dramatists; Olivia Laing; P. Carl; Paul Rusconi; piece by piece productions; Portland Center Stage; Rachel Aedan; Rattlestick Playwrights Theater; Rebecca Taichman; Riccardo Hernandez; Robbie Baitz; Robina Foundation; Sarah Benson, John Selzer, Jon Dembrow, Raphael Martin, Cynthia Flowers and everyone at Soho Repertory Theatre; Stephanie Ward; Stephen Willems and MCC Playwrights' Coalition; Steve Rattazzi; Christopher Hibma, Philip Himberg and Sundance Theatre Lab; Suzanne Scanlon; Anne Washburn and Gordon Dahlquist. Special thanks to Kip Fagan for his incisive, dedicated work on *3C* over the course of several workshops. And to my lawyers at Davis Wright Tremaine: Bruce Johnson, Camille Calman, and the late Ed Davis. And to my excellent indispensable assistant, Philip Gates, who assisted me on both of these plays. And to all the actors who participated in countless readings, workshops, etc., of these plays who aren't mentioned here.

These plays were written and developed with support from the Guggenheim Foundation, the Helen Merrill Foundation, the Bush Foundation, the Jerome Foundation, the Whiting Foundation, the MacDowell Colony, the McKnight Foundation, and the Mellon Foundation.

## Production History

*Marie Antoinette* had its first public performance as a co-production by the Yale Repertory Theatre (James Bundy, Artistic Director; Victoria Nolan, Managing Director) and the American Repertory Theater (Diane Paulus, Artistic Director; William Russo, Managing Director) at the American Repertory Theater in Cambridge, Massachusetts, on September 1, 2012. The performance was directed by Rebecca Taichman, with sets by Riccardo Hernandez, costumes by Gabriel Berry, lighting by Christopher Akerlind, sound by Matt Hubbs, choreography by Karole Armitage, and puppetry design by Matt Acheson. The production stage manager was Amanda Spooner. The cast was as follows:

| | |
|---|---|
| MARIE ANTOINETTE | Brooke Bloom |
| LOUIS XVI | Steven Rattazzi |
| JOSEPH/MR. SAUCE | Fred Arsenault |
| AXEL FERSEN | Jake Silbermann |
| THE DAUPHIN | Andrew Cekala |
| YOLANDE DE POLIGNAC/MRS. SAUCE | Hannah Cabell |
| THÉRÈSE DE LAMBALLE | Polly Lee |
| SHEEP | David Greenspan |
| ROYALIST | Vin Knight |

| | |
|---|---|
| MARIE'S COTERIE | Jo Lampert, Teale Sperling |
| GUARD | Brian Wiles |

*Marie Antoinette* began performances at the Yale Repertory Theatre in New Haven, Connecticut, on October 26, 2012, with the same artistic team. The cast was as follows:

| | |
|---|---|
| MARIE ANTOINETTE | Marin Ireland |
| LOUIS XVI | Steven Rattazzi |
| JOSEPH/MR. SAUCE | Fred Arsenault |
| AXEL FERSEN | Jake Silbermann |
| THE DAUPHIN | Ashton Woerz |
| YOLANDE DE POLIGNAC/MRS. SAUCE | Hannah Cabell |
| THÉRÈSE DE LAMBALLE | Polly Lee |
| SHEEP | David Greenspan |
| ROYALIST | Vin Knight |
| MARIE'S COTERIE | Jo Lampert, Teale Sperling |
| GUARD | Brian Wiles |

The New York premiere of *Marie Antoinette* was produced by Soho Rep. (Sarah Benson, Artistic Director; Cynthia Flowers, Executive Director) and John Adrian Selzer, in association with the American Repertory Theater and Yale Repertory Theatre at Soho Rep. on October 9, 2013. The production was directed by Rebecca Taichman, with sets by Riccardo Hernandez, costumes by Anka Lupes, lighting by Stephen Strawbridge, sound by Matt Hubbs, wigs by Amanda Miller, and choreography by Sam Pinkleton. The production stage manager was Amanda Spooner. The cast was as follows:

| | |
|---|---|
| MARIE ANTOINETTE | Marin Ireland |
| LOUIS XVI | Steven Rattazzi |

| | |
|---|---|
| JOSEPH/MR. SAUCE | Karl Miller |
| AXEL FERSEN | Chris Stack |
| THE DAUPHIN | Aimée Laurence |
| YOLANDE DE POLIGNAC/MRS. SAUCE | Marsha Stephanie Blake |
| THÉRÈSE DE LAMBALLE/ROYALIST | Jennifer Ikeda |
| SHEEP | David Greenspan |
| REVOLUTIONARY | Will Pullen |

## Characters

MARIE ANTOINETTE: Queen of France

LOUIS XVI: Her husband

JOSEPH: Her brother

AXEL FERSEN: A family friend she's attracted to

THE DAUPHIN: Her ten-year-old son

YOLANDE DE POLIGNAC: A false friend

THÉRÈSE DE LAMBALLE: A true friend

MR. SAUCE: A shopkeeper (can double with Joseph)

MRS. SAUCE: His wife (can double with Polignac)

A SHEEP

ROYALIST

REVOLUTIONARY 1, 2 AND 3 (can all be played by one man)

TWO GUARDS (double with Revolutionary and Joseph)


## Mise-en-Place

Versailles, Paris and environs.
1770s–1790s.

## SET

A guillotine.
A palace.
A carriage.
Trianon and le Hameau.
Tuileries and the Jardin.
Tower of the Temple.
Conciergerie.

## Note on Text

I write for the musicality of the line, not grammatical correctness.

The rhythms of the play are not naturalistic. Please don't naturalize them. The play has a honed instability, like Romantic music, a kind of rubato.

A double slash ( // ) indicates either an overlap or a jump—i.e., no break between the end of one character's speech and the beginning of the following speech.

Speech in parentheses indicates either a sidetracked thought—or footnote—within a conversation, or a shift in emphasis with no transition.

When a "?" is followed by a lowercase word, that means you ask the question and keep talking without taking a beat after the question mark.

Sometimes sentences will abut with no period or punctuation This means you just keep talking without taking a beat for a period or comma.

A [STOP] is a *(Pause)* followed by either a marked shift in tone or tempo (like a cinematic jump-cut or a quantum leap) or *no* change in tempo whatsoever—somewhat like putting a movie on pause and then pressing play. These moments in the play are less psychological than energetic. They have a kind of focused yet unpredictable stillness—like martial arts, where there is preparedness in the silence; where a lunge or a swift kick can be delivered from seemingly out of nowhere—quickly, invisibly.

# Marie Antoinette

(1789)

When she walks through your bedrooms carrying butcher knives you'll know the truth.

—Heiner Müller, *Hamletmachine*

# ACT ONE

## 1.

TITLE: 1776

*Marie, Polignac, and Lamballe are taking tea in a palace. They have enormous hair.*

POLIGNAC *(Pouring)*: Tea?
MARIE: (Thanks I'll have a spot) *Oh my god* I'm picking up British affectations "I'll have a spot" //
LAMBALLE: And look what's happening in the colonies //
MARIE: Boston, I *know* //
POLIGNAC: Bedlam.
MARIE: It's crazy, and all for a spot of tea.
POLIGNAC: I hate British people, I have to say;
MARIE: Lafayette writes me letters—
POLIGNAC: Milk?

MARIE: (Yes please) But nobody speaks of revolution here have you noticed?

LAMBALLE *(Opening a case)*: *Cachou?*

MARIE: (No thanks) The people aren't happy; Or—I don't know what they are //

LAMBALLE: There's riots.

MARIE: Are there?

POLIGNAC: But there's always riots //

MARIE: Maybe they are starving. I hear things, but then I think maybe it's all a canard? Human relations are so confusing, they should be transparent and they aren't //

POLIGNAC: That's true //

MARIE: And anyway one hears a number of things, there's sort of a din everywhere—well in France—it's like dishes clattering and breaking everywhere you go, have you noticed?

LAMBALLE: I know,

MARIE: These rumors It hurts my head.

POLIGNAC: We have aspirin,

LAMBALLE: Have you heard of this Rousseau?

MARIE: Who's that.

LAMBALLE: I keep hearing his name, whispers, I don't know. He writes books.

POLIGNAC: We should have him to court.

MARIE: Uch intellectuals blech *(Sips)* you know what I love, *mops!*

LAMBALLE: Mops? //

MARIE: Those little lapdogs with snub noses?

POLIGNAC: That baroness What's her name //

MARIE: Yes //

POLIGNAC: She has a couple //

MARIE: Yes and we have hundreds of them in a room somewhere in the palace,

LAMBALLE: You do? //

MARIE: (Well I can't ever find it) but I hear the barking Little echoes //

POLIGNAC: Cats are more dignified than dogs.

LAMBALLE: You think?

POLIGNAC: Lick the chops, swallow it down, to me it's crude.

MARIE: I don't think so,

POLIGNAC: Well, every once in a while there's an exception.

MARIE: Exceptions prove rules! That's what my governess at Schönbrunn said.

LAMBALLE: In Austria?

MARIE: Countess Brandeis—

POLIGNAC: Do you miss Austria, Marie?

MARIE: Well I had 124 kitchens, that was pretty interesting.

POLIGNAC: And how many in Versailles?

MARIE: You know I've never seen it all—I always take a wrong turn and end up going in circles (*Laughs; sips*) Vienna has the best pastries though //

POLIGNAC: Really //

MARIE: The linzer tarts omigod //

POLIGNAC: But you're so skinny.

MARIE (*Showing off*): Yes and I dispensed with whalebone too.

POLIGNAC: You did *not*.

MARIE: It was giving me *welts*!

POLIGNAC: You're not wearing your *corset*?!

LAMBALLE: I feel sorry for the whales.

POLIGNAC: Marie you're scandalous.

MARIE: But I set the fashions //

LAMBALLE: That's true.

POLIGNAC: But it isn't seemly—

MARIE: Seemly is relative: because of me hairdos got so high they had to raise the roofs of carriages, what was *that*.

POLIGNAC: What does Louis say?

MARIE: Oh we're always in fights,

LAMBALLE: Same old? //

MARIE: I do like to disport myself I'm sorry, even buffeted by the outcries of peasants—I'm a queen I cannot simply forfeit my luxuries.

LAMBALLE: No it'd be calamitous.

MARIE *(Sighs)*: And *Versailles* //

POLIGNAC *(Sympathy)*: (Darling:) //

MARIE *(Rapid shift)*: There's all these FUCKING rules I can't TAKE IT (I-mean-I-know-I'm-acting-all-victimized—) //

POLIGNAC: *(No)* //

MARIE: But do you know what it's like having people watch you dress, undress, eat dinner *every night* Like you're some *specimen*?

POLIGNAC: It's so invasive //

MARIE: *Invasive?* they should just press me between glass *slides*.

LAMBALLE: What are you going to do?

MARIE: I told Louis I need a new palace (I'm calling it Trianon) //

POLIGNAC: You're kidding //

MARIE: I'll live there and take my entertainments as well, and I'll have my dinner *alone* thanks //

POLIGNAC: And Louis *agreed*?! //

MARIE: (Or with friends) *what* NO (Well there was a fracas The chords in his neck got all tight but I won in the end) //

LAMBALLE: The courtiers'll be quite angry.

MARIE *(Punctuated with rage at the end)*: Yes I expect, but it's too bad; people aren't meant to live this way it's SUFFOCATING ME.

*(A long silence.)*

POLIGNAC *(Damage control)*: Then you did the right thing //

MARIE: (But I do have ministrations Things like that I'm not some apostate) //

LAMBALLE: No one's saying that.

MARIE *(Tiny beat)*: You're kind. But I know people think I'm very bad.

*(Long uncomfortable pause.)*

POLIGNAC *(Too bright)*: No.

*(Long uncomfortable pause.)*

LAMBALLE: One mustn't make too much of one's reputation.

[STOP]

MARIE: What's in this one Is it apricot? //

LAMBALLE: It's very toothsome really //

POLIGNAC: I'm such a hypocrite: My kids love junk They're always after me to buy them sweets You know cakes and things But I make them eat healthy Then I gorge at parties //

MARIE: Oh let them eat cake //

POLIGNAC: Isn't sugar bad for their teeth?

MARIE: You think they won't sneak it? //

POLIGNAC: That's true //

MARIE: *Try the ganache* //

LAMBALLE: It's good right?

*(They eat.)*

MARIE *(Eating)*: In Vienna I used to just have an espresso every day in the morning for breakfast, and like a piece of chocolate and a biscuit and that was it. And nobody stood around *watching* me eat, I just ate. And I didn't have to look at my reflection all day in gilt-edged mirrors I was outside, in nature, playing. The oak trees, the firs All that sunlight? The pores of my skin drank up sunlight.

*(Beat.)*

French people don't appreciate nature.

POLIGNAC: Go to the Bois de Boulogne.

MARIE: It's not the same thing, I'm talking about *nature*! //

POLIGNAC: How is it not the same thing! //

MARIE: That's a *park*, It's man-*made*—I've been to the Bois de Boulogne OK it's not what I'm talking about.

LAMBALLE: Qu'est-ce que c'est?

MARIE: I don't know; I miss those shepherds in the mountains, the sound of the Danube rolling by,

POLIGNAC *(Derision in this)*: You're so *Austrian*.

*(Beat.)*

MARIE *(Stung)*: Is that a *bad* thing?

*(Eek.)*

POLIGNAC: I'm not saying it's a bad // thing.

MARIE *(Mustering imperiousness)*: I AM Austrian.

*(Long uncomfortable pause.)*

LAMBALLE *(Buffering)*: And look how flawless your French is.

*(Beat.)*

MARIE: It's all in the gullet
right here
back of the throat.
*(She rolls an "R")*
See?

*(Polignac imitates her. Marie corrects her. Polignac tries once more. Then Lamballe gives it a go.*
*They all do it.)*

[STOP]

*(They look at each other—see the ridiculousness of it—they burst out laughing.*
*Pageantry, flourish; a masked ball, a quadrille.)*

# 2.

TITLE: VERSAILLES

*The palace is a mess.*
*There's lots of watches and clock parts everywhere.*
*Louis is in pajamas, wig unkempt, playing with a clock.*
*Marie is being dressed; it is incredibly processional.*

MARIE: Clocks undone, watch springs everywhere You're like a little boy //
LOUIS: Well I never had a childhood //
MARIE: (Don't whine) //
LOUIS: I like to take things apart and see how they work //
MARIE: That can be dangerous—
LOUIS: Hobbies are fun //
MARIE: And it's a lot of broken clocks Can't you clean this?

12

LOUIS: No.

MARIE: This place is a mess.

LOUIS: You make messes too you know //

MARIE *(Examining the swatch of fabric)*: But I hate any mess that isn't mine, you know that What time is it (ooh I like these little striations look) //

LOUIS: Eight.

MARIE: What //

LOUIS: EIGHT //

MARIE *(Looks at a clock)*: It says four.

LOUIS: I'll fix that.

MARIE: Has it ever occurred to you to *run France*?

LOUIS: Why do you have so much contempt for me?

MARIE: It's your lassitude.

LOUIS: Do you know what DAY it is?

MARIE: Thursday?

LOUIS: It's my *birthday*.

MARIE: You expect me to remember that?

LOUIS: Yes!

MARIE: I have *fifteen* brothers and sisters, I can hardly remember their *names* //

LOUIS: I'm your *husband* //

MARIE: We're great friends you and I
Let's not mar it with facts (By the way I need some money) //

LOUIS: Marie: this heedless // extravagance

MARIE: It's not heedless *Look* at me //

LOUIS: What:

MARIE: What do you mean *what*— This dress?!

LOUIS: What's wrong with that dress?

MARIE: Are you *kidding*?
*Moths* wouldn't eat it.

LOUIS: Why do you go to the trouble of speaking to me, just send me an invoice.

MARIE: In care of: //

LOUIS (*Hurt*): You're so *mean.*

MARIE: Did you sleep well //

LOUIS (*Tantrum*): NO!

MARIE: You're cranky, go play with your clocks (Too much // rouge)

LOUIS: *Meanie* //

MARIE: And your wig's uncombed You should // fix it

LOUIS: And it wouldn't hurt to wear a corset or stays //

MARIE: "Stays" //

LOUIS: That's what girls wear! //

MARIE: You're so quotidian.

(*Beat.*)

LOUIS (*Returns to his clocks, quiet*): Where are you going anyway?

MARIE: See some // friends.

(*The clocks start gonging simultaneously over her response; it's a bit chaotic as he tries to silence the various clocks.*)

LOUIS: "WHAT?"

MARIE: "I'M //

LOUIS: ONE SECOND.

MARIE (*Over gongs*): WHAT THE HELL ARE YOU DOING?

LOUIS: IT'S AN EXPERIMENT AND DON'T SWEAR.

MARIE: YOU HAVE TO GROW UP.

LOUIS: WHAT?

(*He stops the gonging.*)

MARIE: I SAID YOU HAVE TO—

(*Beat.*)

*(Quiet, serious)* You have to grow up.

*(Beat; tone shifts.)*

LOUIS: It was just an experiment.
I was // seeing if
MARIE: My mother bore sixteen children
I've bore none.

*(Beat.)*

LOUIS *(Adolescent shrug)*: So.
MARIE: So when are you going to give me a child.
LOUIS *(Averting his gaze)*: Are you in competition with your mother?
MARIE: I am in competition with everyone.
LOUIS: Very funny—
MARIE: Don't deflect.

*(Beat.)*

LOUIS: You know about *(Whispers) the problem.*
MARIE: The people are clamoring for an heir //
LOUIS: Well I don't know what I should do.
MARIE: You spoke to the doctor.
LOUIS: SHHH //
MARIE: Well you did!
LOUIS: Maybe it'll just resolve itself!
MARIE: It's been seven *years*. There's a lot of animus towards me They're saying I'm barren.
LOUIS: I don't *want* to get an operation.
MARIE: It's very minor.
LOUIS *(Tiny, sad)*: It's my penis.
MARIE: Will you stop acting like a baby // I'm

LOUIS: *You* get an operation See how you like it //
MARIE *(To herself, exiting)*: Oh my god Forget it.
LOUIS: I'M ORDERING YOU NOT TO SWEAR

*(She exits.)*

*(Hurt, deflated)* Where are you going?

3.

*Late night promenade, Bois de Boulogne.*
*We hear fireworks in the distance and see, sporadically, the glare.*
*Marie and Fersen are alone.*

FERSEN *(Takes Marie's fan)*: What's this?
MARIE *(Takes it back)*: Fragonard.

*(She flicks it open.)*

FERSEN: Ooh la la very fancy.
MARIE: Well they do call me *the butterfly queen.*

*(She fans herself, does a little spin, "flutters," trips, laughs at herself; Fersen catches her. It's suddenly tense.)*

FERSEN: Watch out little butterfly or I'll catch you in my nets.

MARIE: What'll you do.

FERSEN: Pin you to the wall;

MARIE: Then I'll scream—

FERSEN: Butterflies can't scream They just beat their little impaled wings //

MARIE: And then they get pressed in a book and forgotten That's a sad end.

FERSEN: That's life.

MARIE *(Disentangling herself from him)*: Nice epaulets.

FERSEN: How're things at home?

MARIE: Louis thinks you're ignoring him.

FERSEN: Doesn't he know we're having an affair.

MARIE: We're not.

*(Pause.)*

FERSEN: Aren't we?

*(Beat.)*

MARIE: No.

FERSEN: Seems a waste.

[STOP]

MARIE: Look I'm attracted to // you:

FERSEN: And it's // mutual

MARIE: But I'm married and people talk //

FERSEN: Not that you care a whit.

MARIE *(Posture straightening)*: *Don't* I.

*(Pause.)*

FERSEN: That's
that's not the impression I get.

*(Beat.)*

MARIE *(Regal, distant)*: Your impressions are mistakenly formed.

*(Beat.)*

FERSEN: Are you happy?

*(Pause.)*

MARIE *(Resisting him)*: You're forgetting your station.

*(Fersen retracts, embarrassed; looks up at the fireworks; awkward silence.)*

FERSEN: Look.
All the colors.

*(Fireworks; more silence.)*

MARIE: The night Louis and I were married
there was a violent thunderstorm
and they had to cancel the fireworks
and it's been like that ever since.

*(She looks at him; beat.)*

FERSEN: What are you going to do?

*(Pause; Marie transfixes her gaze on the fireworks; she's desperate to stay composed.)*

MARIE: I'm a little bit trapped I'm afraid.

*(Pause.)*

FERSEN: It's a lovely night.

*(Silence; pace slackens.)*

MARIE *(A part of her that's untouched)*: Ten years from now how will you remember me.
FERSEN: Like this:
MARIE: How.
FERSEN: A butterfly with opalescent wings.

*(Marie says nothing; we hear the fireworks.)*

Is that bad?
MARIE: No.
FERSEN: What's the matter?
MARIE *(Gazing absently at the glare in the sky)*: Nothing. *(Pause)* Sometimes I feel like a game that other people play but without me. It's kind of lonely actually.

*(Pause.)*

FERSEN: You feel used?
MARIE: Is that what I mean?
FERSEN: Don't you know?
MARIE *(Being truthful)*: No.
  *(After a beat)* I'm tired.

*(She rises.)*

Three feet of hair is a workout I must say, I get neckaches.

*(She kisses him on the cheek.)*

I'll have to speak to Leonard about it //
FERSEN: Who //
MARIE: My hairdresser; maybe I'll chop it all off.

*(The sounds of a horse-drawn carriage.)*

Call me.

*(She disappears into the carriage.)*

4.

TITLE: 1777

*Palace of Versailles.*
*Joseph is berating his sister.*

JOSEPH: You are a queen by right and // by destiny
MARIE: Do you want me to cut you up a pear // or something
JOSEPH: You rule by divine *right* // and it's
MARIE: *Yes* //
JOSEPH: Not merely a right it's a // responsi*bility*
MARIE: Yes I know THAT Joseph what's this all about really //
JOSEPH: You //
MARIE: "LOUIS IS THAT YOU?" (I think he's hiding in the
    antechamber he's very afraid of you) I'm sorry you were
    saying:

*(An indignant pause.)*

(Sorry.)

JOSEPH: Mother is very concerned //

MARIE: About: //

JOSEPH: MARIE! //

MARIE: Yes?

*(Beat.)*

JOSEPH: You are an amiable young woman //

MARIE: (thanks) //

JOSEPH: who never thinks of anything but her amusements, her dresses, her daily // pastimes

MARIE *(Temper flaring momentarily)*: THAT'S SUCH // BULLSHIT

JOSEPH: You never read //

MARIE *(Quick)*: (Because I hate reading I have very poor // concentration)

JOSEPH: You never hear *anyone* talk sense for a quarter of an hour during a // whole month, never

MARIE: That's not // true

TITLE: A SHEEP ENTERS THE ROOM

*(A Sheep enters the room, looks at Marie. She clocks the sheep, who then turns and exits. Marie is the only one who can see it.)*

JOSEPH: think anything out, and, I am *certain*: *never* give a moment's reflection to the consequences of anything you—

*(Joseph follows her gaze, nothing. She appears completely abstracted.)*

ANTOINE!!!!!

MARIE: Did you see that?

JOSEPH: *You're not listening //* to me.

MARIE: You didn't just see a sheep?

JOSEPH: I'M SPEAKING!

MARIE *(Impatient)*: Well I think it's a bit weird that a *sheep* just crossed the room, I thought it warranted a footnote in the conversation.

JOSEPH: You're hopeless //

MARIE *(Taut)*: Yes I'm inept at being a queen—I have bad penmanship I'm illiterate You supersede me in *all* respects Joseph //

JOSEPH: I'm //

MARIE: You're amazing and I'm shit //

JOSEPH: I'm not *saying //* that

MARIE: That's what it YES YOU ARE—and I hate being *patronized* and now // sheep are

JOSEPH: When are you going to produce an *heir*?

*(Pause.)*

MARIE: I don't know.

JOSEPH: What do you mean "you don't // know"

MARIE: You'll have to take it up with Louis.

JOSEPH: It's been seven years

Are you barren? //

MARIE: That's none of your fucking business //

JOSEPH: It's very *much* my business.

MARIE: Is this some kind of espionage?

JOSEPH: Mother is very concerned, you're childless, you spend too much money //

MARIE: I think I've // been

JOSEPH: Your methods of ruling are heterodox to say the least //

MARIE: That has nothing to do with me, that's Louis' fault and he's crazy, he acts like he's twelve, he's INCAPABLE of making up his mind—

JOSEPH: What are you saying Antoine That mother made a bad *match*? //

MARIE: Don't be naive. Mother doesn't make "matches" she engineers *political* alliances—and this one's turning out to be a long suck on a dry prune frankly!

JOSEPH: I won't have you speak of mother that way!

MARIE: (Oh calm down.)

JOSEPH: You have very bad manners //

MARIE: So I've heard.

*(Pause; an impasse.)*

*(Conciliating)* How's.
Austria—doing.

JOSEPH: Fine.

*(Beat.)*

MARIE: You like being emperor?

JOSEPH: It's fine.

MARIE: I'll tell you I miss Schönbrunn.
I do, Countess Brandeis; how is she?

JOSEPH: I don't consort with Countess Brandeis.

MARIE: I miss having a governess.
I wonder if she thinks of me.

*(Pause.)*

Well if you do run into her
send her my love. Would you?

JOSEPH: Sure.

MARIE: She was lovely, she always let me skip my homework.

*(Beat.)*

Chocolate?

JOSEPH: No thank you.

MARIE: Parisian chocolates are lovely.

*(She pops one herself, chews contemplatively.)*

Do you ever think about that Joseph? Schönbrunn, when we were kids, and oh I don't know. Just. *(He isn't responsive)* I mean it sounds stupid but—being wild, and carefree, and playing in the mountains and singing songs?

JOSEPH: "Songs."

*(Beat.)*

MARIE *(Deflating)*: No. You wouldn't have time for that.

JOSEPH *(Dismissive)*: Uh. Not *really*.

*(Beat.)*

MARIE *(Real pain—she can't cap it here)*: Well
    I'm sure you think I'm being *frivolous* but
    It's been hard for me.
    I've had to take leave of everything Austrian
    Every stitch on my back, did you know that?
    And I *miss* things, I was only fourteen when I came here.

JOSEPH: Everyone makes sacrifices.

*(Pause.)*

MARIE *(Numb)*: I guess.

*(Pause.)*

I do appreciate you coming by Joseph
I know I'm considered "difficult"
and this is all for my own good //
JOSEPH: You're the Queen of France.
MARIE: I know.
JOSEPH: Mother is very *concerned.*
MARIE: And I want to dispel her fears—truly—

*(Louis peeks in; gets scared.)*

Louis—there he is—you can come in it's all right.
JOSEPH *(Looks around, confused)*: Louis?
MARIE: You can come in, he's not going to bite you (I don't
know why he's so afraid of you, I'll get him) "LOUIS!"

*(She goes out into the hall. They have a row. Louis enters,
Marie enters behind him. Louis is terribly nervous, he's shaking and sweating.)*

LOUIS: Hello Joseph //
MARIE *(Fixing his unkempt wig)*: (Stand up straight) //
JOSEPH: Marie and I were just talking about you.
LOUIS: Oh you were?
JOSEPH: About why you two haven't produced an heir.
LOUIS *(Feigned deafness)*: I'm
    I'm
    I'm *sorry?*
JOSEPH: An HEIR?

*(Beat.)*

LOUIS: Pardon me, do you have a handkerchief? I'm very hot.

JOSEPH: Are you impotent?

LOUIS: Am I //

JOSEPH: Marie says she isn't barren, so I'm just wondering if you're impotent. I'm sorry to be so forthright, it's just that, well we feel that seven years is a sufficient amount of time to wait for an heir.

LOUIS: Yes, I see.

MARIE: (He's not // impotent)

LOUIS (*Hysterical*): IS HE TALKING TO YOU?

(*Joseph looks at him dispassionately.*)

JOSEPH: I know this must be very sensitive // for you.

LOUIS: *Tell her to stop looking at me.*

(*Pause.*)

The thing is
Joseph
I get very—healthy erections.

(*They look at him.*)

There's just a problem getting the
the "stuff" out.

(*They look at him.*)

JOSEPH: "Stuff."

LOUIS: The. I //

MARIE: He needs to have a minor operation //

LOUIS (*Tantrum*): IT'S-NOT-MINOR.

*(He looks at Joseph. Smiles anxiously.)*

JOSEPH: Is that all it is?
MARIE: He keeps putting it off.
JOSEPH: Why don't you just have it?
LOUIS: Because
     they
     they cut you down there.
JOSEPH: Can't you just be a brave little man?

*(Louis smiles, tries not to weep.)*

MARIE: Please be reasonable.
     Don't you want children?

*(Louis weeps quietly, nods.)*

JOSEPH: Louis.

*(Pause.)*

LOUIS: I'm very embarrassed.
JOSEPH: Don't be embarrassed it's OK.
     Now come with me.
LOUIS: Where are we going?
JOSEPH: Don't be frightened.

*(He mouths "I'm taking him to the doctor" to Marie; she gets all excited. Joseph and Louis exit.)*

LOUIS *(On exiting)*: Have you seen my clocks? //
JOSEPH: Do you foxhunt? //
LOUIS: I've got watchsprings.

## 5.

*Marie and Polignac, dressed as shepherdesses, are surveying the grounds of le Hameau.*
*Fake pastoralism.*
*Herds of sheep grazing; there should be something ersatz about it.*
*Marie's enormous spires of hair are now shorn, cut tight in "l'enfant" hairstyle, as is Polignac's.*

MARIE: Tilly, my page, she's so sweet, she says I walk better than any other woman //

POLIGNAC: I love Tilly! //

MARIE: And just as you'd offer a regular person a chair you'd offer me a throne!

POLIGNAC: Awww //

MARIE: Her parents were serfs //

POLIGNAC: (There's still something of that in her)

MARIE: She pays compliments very naturally //

POLIGNAC: I love nature!

MARIE: I told you!

(*Points*) See the cracks in the wood that's very authentic right? The first time it looked very fake I had them do it over; and we installed this fabulous farming couple from Touraine, they do all the cheese, the dairy //

POLIGNAC: It's so cozy //

MARIE: I know I love the simplicity of it, this is all I really need //

POLIGNAC: Is that a windmill? //

MARIE (*Pouring water into bowls*): All those mirrors, those gilded things, I'm done!

POLIGNAC: What's that? //

MARIE: Sèvres porcelain.

POLIGNAC: I'm supposed to drink from this?

MARIE: It's more peasanty.

(*They sip.*)

I used my own breasts as a mold, it adds to the fun I thought.

(*Polignac chokes.*)

POLIGNAC (*Bright*): Oh!

MARIE: Helen of Troy did that; she's my inspiration!

POLIGNAC: I love *The Odyssey*.

(*Beat.*)

MARIE (*Clueless*): What's that?

POLIGNAC: By Homer?

(*Pause.*)

MARIE (*Brazen ignorance*): Who?

*(Double-take.)*

POLIGNAC: *H*omer?

*(Marie looks at her with a blank expression.)*

[STOP]

*(Stymied) I love your brooch //*
MARIE: I'm doing bows now, simplicity, clean lines, nothing too
ornate, metals—no big jewels—organic flowing forms //
POLIGNAC: White organdy //
MARIE: *Exactement //*
POLIGNAC *(Inhales)*: And it smells lovely //
MARIE: I have the goats and sheep perfumed, I don't like rustic
smells //
POLIGNAC: That's clever //
MARIE: Do you want to play roulette later I feel like gambling.
POLIGNAC: I don't have much money with me //
MARIE *(Rapt)*: You SEE: THIS is what I love, you're so SIMPLE.
I just want an uncomplicated life—I'm wholesome!—
I feel so misunderstood.

*(She feeds a goat.)*

POLIGNAC: You really are.

*(Beat.)*

MARIE *(As she feeds the goat)*: We can just use my money.
POLIGNAC: What.
MARIE: For roulette.
POLIGNAC: Marie I couldn't take any more from you.
MARIE: Arrête!
POLIGNAC: But you've already been so generous.

MARIE: That's what friends are for! You know I got Thérèse a
job in the palace Do you want one?

POLIGNAC: Like what?

MARIE *(Coy)*: Governess?

POLIGNAC: Are you *pregnant?*

MARIE: Well: Louis had an operation.

POLIGNAC: Why? Is he all right?

MARIE: I shouldn't be telling you this but he had *(Stage whisper)*
*phimosis.*

POLIGNAC: What's *phimosis?*

MARIE: This rare disease where the orifice of the prepuce contracts when the man gets an erection and then he can't
*re*tract it.

POLIGNAC: Hmm.

MARIE: So everyone's blaming me and saying I'm barren, but
it's not my fault at all (you don't mind my speaking can-
didly do you Duchess) he just had surgery so I hope that
works—"hello Isabelle" //

POLIGNAC: (Who's that?) //

MARIE: (Some peasant girl we installed) //

POLIGNAC: (Sweet) //

MARIE: (She picks flowers) —oh I have to be discreet I don't
want all this to get around!

POLIGNAC: I won't say a word.

MARIE: Thanks; hey, what time is it?

POLIGNAC: Quarter after one //

MARIE: OK so at two there's a vernissage, a friend of Watteau,
Thérèse said she'd meet us there.

POLIGNAC: I thought you wanted to play roulette.

MARIE: Oh that's right. OK so we'll do the vernissage from
two to three, then kibbitz, then sneak back to Trianon and
play roulette.

*(A Sheep has sidled up to Marie.)*

POLIGNAC: I think that sheep likes you:

MARIE: What, oh;

SHEEP: Baaaa.

MARIE: "Nice sheep."

*(She pets it.)*

POLIGNAC: That sheep really likes you.

*(The Sheep nuzzles Marie.)*

MARIE *(Pretending not to be uncomfortable)*: Well this is how it is in nature, untrammeled affection, that's just par for the course.

SHEEP: Baaaa.

POLIGNAC: Where's the dairy I feel like making myself a cheese plate,

MARIE: Haven't you had lunch //

POLIGNAC: No //

MARIE: Oh you must be famished //

POLIGNAC: And maybe a glass of bordeaux? //

MARIE: Make a left at the windmill, and then turn right, you'll see a row of run-down shacks and then there's the dairy—

POLIGNAC: Do you want me to bring you something?

MARIE: That's fine I'll wait here:

POLIGNAC: OK //

SHEEP *(Nuzzling Marie neurotically)*: Baaa //

MARIE *(Pets the lamb perfunctorily)*: Or maybe actually a SLIVER of vacherin and some water crackers //

POLIGNAC: That sheep's really into you //

MARIE: But just a sliver I'm on a diet //

POLIGNAC: OK.

*(Polignac exits.*
*The Sheep looks at Marie. Marie looks back, uncomfortable.*
*They look at each other.)*

MARIE *(Makes a face)*: What what are you *looking at*?!

SHEEP: Comment allez-vous?

MARIE *(Jumps)*: OH MY GOD.

SHEEP: Baaa.

MARIE: Who are you?

SHEEP: A sheep.

MARIE: You're the sheep from the other day!

SHEEP: Oui.

MARIE: Do we know each other?

SHEEP: You remember me Antoine.

MARIE: Antoine That's what the Hapsburgs call me.

SHEEP: From Austria?

MARIE *(Reluctant; a beat)*: I. Don't know any sheep from Austria; *(Reasserting a regal stance)* And the Duchess de Polignac will be back any //

SHEEP: Pet me.

MARIE *(Thrown)*: What.

SHEEP: Please pet me.

*(The Sheep bats his eyelashes.)*

MARIE *(Looks around, embarrassed)*: I pet you already.

*(The Sheep bats his eyelashes.)*

Go—graze or something—

*(They look at each other. The Sheep smiles at her.)*

You're very recalcitrant.

SHEEP: I like to be pet lots.

*(She reluctantly pets him.)*

MARIE: You're very fleecy.

SHEEP: You can shear me too.

MARIE: That'd be nice, then I'd be like a real shepherdess.

SHEEP: Baaa.

MARIE: How do you like *le Hameau*?

SHEEP: It's nice.

MARIE: Were you out grazing? It's peaceful here isn't it? Don't you think it's like Austria?

SHEEP: Marie:

MARIE: What is it Sheep?

SHEEP: I thought I should share something with you.

*(The Sheep opens his mouth. Marie pulls out a piece of rolled parchment.)*

MARIE: Oh!

What's this. It's a poem.

SHEEP: Read it.

MARIE: OK.

*(Reads:)*

"There once was a queen named Marie"

*(Beams)*

Oh that's so *sweet*.

SHEEP: Baaa.

MARIE: "There once was a queen named Marie Who'd lick her own cunt while she'd pee—"

*(Beat.)*

*(Face contorts)* Oh.

That isn't very nice.

SHEEP: Keep reading:

*(She looks at the Sheep. The Sheep looks back at her innocently, shrugs.)*

36

MARIE *(Continues)*: "They'd tell her 'your grace
    You've got pee on your face'
    And she'd piss herself laughing with—"

*(Beat.)*

    That's disgusting Where'd you get this?
SHEEP: Sorry.
MARIE: Who's writing these things?
SHEEP: Everyone; you should be careful;
MARIE: Of what?
SHEEP: The people are very angry //
MARIE: Oh they're always angry that's not a barometer of anything.
SHEEP: They're starving, and they're over-taxed //
MARIE: That's Louis' problem, he's working on it //
SHEEP: Baaaaa.
MARIE: Anyway this obloquy can't hurt me.
    *(She crumples up the parchment)*
    Besides I was ridiculed for my extravagances but I'm done with all that. I've given up fashion.
SHEEP: There are pamphlets circulating that say you gave blowjobs to an entire guards regiment in a single night.

[STOP]

MARIE *(Feigning control)*: Well. At least they credit me with virtuosity.
SHEEP: Step carefully.

# 6.

TITLE: TEN YEARS LATER

*Outdoors, Marie and Lamballe, practicing archery.*
*Marie is more modestly dressed than in previous scenes.*

MARIE: I'm having a change of heart.
LAMBALLE: About what?
MARIE: I don't know, everything.
    I think things are taking a turn for the better.
    I'm still keeping those Records.
LAMBALLE: Which?
MARIE: My spending's way down //
LAMBALLE: You're keeping records?
MARIE: *I told you that.*
LAMBALLE *(Flummoxed)*: When?

MARIE: I cut my spending in half. I keep my receipts,
    I have this little ledger and everything.
LAMBALLE: This is incredible!
MARIE: I don't know if the rest of
    France thinks it's so great.
    Your turn:

*(Lamballe's turn. A short pause as she deliberates whether to
speak.)*

LAMBALLE *(Forced nonchalance)*: That uh. Woman . . . escaped
    prison.
MARIE: Who?
LAMBALLE: Lamotte.
MARIE: Ugh Enough with the *necklace* already!

*(An uncomfortable pause.)*

LAMBALLE *(Demurring)*: Uh. Yes well She's. She's telling every-
    one you're a lesbian and that you two had this . . . lesbian
    affair.
MARIE: She's been saying that for years //
LAMBALLE: But people are starting to believe // it
MARIE: How can I be both a lesbian and blowing the whole
    infantry at Versailles?! //
LAMBALLE: Or //
MARIE: Be *consistent.*
LAMBALLE: (Is there any more gianduja?)
MARIE: (I can get you more) —"Tilly?" //
LAMBALLE: (No that's all right My // figure)
MARIE: I mean I flirt but that's healthy Lots of women flirt.
    *(Beat)* It's in my personality.
LAMBALLE *(Demurring)*: Yes.
MARIE: You think it's too much?

LAMBALLE *(Beat; gingerly)*: Maybe a little prudence isn't a bad thing.

MARIE *("Fun")*: I used a know a girl called Prudence, British, she had *horrible* teeth—

*(Beat.)*

*(Somber)* Yes you're right.

You know me I just hate any kind of constriction.

LAMBALLE: I know //

MARIE: I feel so hemmed in //

LAMBALLE: But you are the queen.

MARIE: Yes I am that. *(Beat)* You're right. I don't know why I'm feeling so defensive; I don't have anything to prove.

LAMBALLE: And then these scurrilous rumors'll be put to rout //

MARIE: Yes //

LAMBALLE *(Sanguine smile)*: And the cartoons.

*(Marie eats a chocolate.)*

MARIE: Yes.

*(Stops chewing)*

What cartoons.

LAMBALLE *(Trying to make it go away)*: I've *heard*

I haven't seen // them.

MARIE: Bullshit What are they of //

LAMBALLE: I haven't seen them Marie I // swear—

MARIE: Oh *bullshit*!

LAMBALLE: One hears things.

[STOP]

MARIE *(Panic)*: What else?

LAMBALLE *(Playing dumb)*: What do you mean?

MARIE: You're such a bad liar Stop it.

*(Beat.)*

LAMBALLE: OK.
There's an autobiography circulating //
MARIE: By whom?
LAMBALLE: *You* supposedly and // you're
MARIE: *Me* //
LAMBALLE: Yeah and you're confessing all your "sins" //
MARIE: "Sins"?
LAMBALLE: From when you were a prostitute?

*(Marie laughs. She stops. Lamballe's not joking.*
*She holds her head, a migraine's coming on.)*

MARIE *(Quiet)*: Why didn't anyone give me a copy of this
did you read it?
LAMBALLE: No //
MARIE: But people have read it
people believe // it
LAMBALLE: It strains credulity;
most people I spoke to // about it
MARIE *(Panic)*: Most? //
LAMBALLE: I //
MARIE: Who have you spoke to?
LAMBALLE: Hardly anyone—

*(Pause.)*

MARIE *(No affect, distant)*: Oh.
OK.
Oh so that's why I haven't seen the
Polignacs, yes I see.

*(Pause.)*

LAMBALLE: A tiny stain on one's // reputation—
MARIE *(Exasperated)*: TINY?
   *(Shift to imperiousness)*
   I'm a *queen* Thérèse not a whore.
   I'll have them branded and
   imprisoned for life.
LAMBALLE: Is that a Good Idea do you // think
MARIE *(Temper)*: No it's not a Good Idea It's an *apotheosis.*
LAMBALLE: Look what happened with the Necklace.

   *(On the word "necklace" Marie freezes.)*

Spare yourself a second humiliation.

   *(Pause. She slumps. She's humbled yet again.)*

MARIE: I don't even know what apotheosis means.
LAMBALLE: It'll blow over;
   be patient.

   *(Beat; she takes a breath, picks up a quiver.)*

MARIE *(Weakly optimistic)*: I'm spending a lot less. That's something,
   Right?
LAMBALLE: It'll blow over You'll see.

   *(Lamballe shoots an arrow.)*

Crap My aim's getting worse.
MARIE: Actually, it's interesting: Louis held me the other night;
   He said "I'm proud of you." He's never said that to me.

LAMBALLE: You see?

*(Beat.)*

MARIE *(Weakly)*: I suppose I am proud of myself.

*(Drifting further and further away, lost.)*

But
I know there's something
else in me that wants to get out.
A little bird beating its wings against
the inside of its cage; it's funny.

*(Sound of a bird flapping its wings, louder and louder.)*

# 7.

TITLE: JUNE 1789

*Palace of Versailles.*
*Marie is strung out. Louis is shuffling through his various dossiers,*
*contracts, etc., in panic. Fersen looks on, attempting to downplay his*
*concern.*

MARIE: Tennis courts are for playing tennis
　　　not swearing oaths //
FERSEN: I agree //
MARIE: (Practicing your // backhand)
LOUIS: Well it's // crazy
FERSEN: And did you hear there are aristocrats
　　　voluntarily turning over their estates
　　　to be redistributed to the peasants //

MARIE: OK well that's a bit much Isn't there some other solution A stopgap?

LOUIS: I'm chary of making any concessions:

MARIE: *No you shouldn't.*

FERSEN: "Give them an // inch"

LOUIS: Or maybe it's a powder keg and I'm helping to foment revolution?!

MARIE: Well then play nice—

LOUIS: I did I met with the assemblies—

MARIE: So:

LOUIS: And it backfired!

FERSEN: So they're not to be trusted.

LOUIS *(Angry)*: They just seem so ANGRY //

MARIE: Yes Well it's a *mob* //

LOUIS *(Insecure)*: Maybe Turgot was right and I should've taxed landed wealth //

MARIE: And then you FIRED him! //

LOUIS *(Tiny)*: You think that was // unjust?

MARIE: I-DON'T-KNOW- // -LOUIS!!!

LOUIS *(Wringing his hands nervously)*: He said if we taxed everyone only a few ducats more that'd avert bankruptcy.

MARIE: We aren't bankrupt.

FERSEN: Actually the public debt has tripled,

MARIE: Since when?

FERSEN: Past few years //

MARIE: *And it's my fault* //

LOUIS: No one's blaming // you

MARIE: They *aren't* What are you in*sensate* You didn't feel the *hostility* in the room?

LOUIS: It was general—

MARIE: It was directed AT ME They're gunning for ME.

*(Pause.)*

I just don't know what these people want from me I'm a
lesbian I'm a prostitute—

LOUIS: You can't please everyone //

MARIE: (You're right and you know what I can't deal with this
my *son* is ill.)

FERSEN: Charles?

MARIE: Joseph he's //

FERSEN: What's wrong?

(*Beat.*)

MARIE: He'll be fine // it's

FERSEN: He's all right?

(*Beat.*)

MARIE: It's just a bit overwhelming.

FERSEN (*Concern*): Is there anything // I can

MARIE (*Attack*): HE'LL BE FINE.

(*Beat.*)

LOUIS: She's under a lot of stress.

FERSEN: I'm on your side Marie.

(*Beat.*)

MARIE (*Relaxes a bit*): Unlike Lafayette
I can't believe he spearheaded this thing.

FERSEN: He's very seduced by American Ideas //

LOUIS (*Snarky*): "America" //

MARIE: That's true he's gone gaga;

FERSEN: But you supported America.

MARIE (*Innocuous*): When?

LOUIS: We signed a treaty.

MARIE *(Tantrum)*: WE-DIDN'T-KNOW-WHAT-THE-HELL-
THAT-WAS-LOUIS //

FERSEN: Uh //

MARIE: Now they're drawing up constitutions on the *tennis court?*

LOUIS: It's // insane

MARIE: They're challenging your divine right to monarchy—
yes it *is* insane—and they're propounding this this //

LOUIS: Why can't we just do something?

MARIE: We what do you mean WE.

LOUIS: Me and you.

MARIE: No not "me and you" I don't have any agency here—I
can't cut down on my clothes anymore I can't wear *burlap*
It's *your* turn to *act.*

*(Louis starts fidgeting, trying to quell panic.)*

LOUIS: I
I. I could call troops?

FERSEN: That's a good idea.

LOUIS: *Really?*

FERSEN: Contain opposition Why not?

*(Beat. He's more emboldened.)*

LOUIS: You know like Troops yeah like get a *concentration* of—
all over Versailles?

*(Pause.
He looks to Fersen for affirmation. He gets nothing.
He looks to Marie for affirmation. He gets nothing.
He bites his nails. He panics.)*

And uh . . . also . . . *(Ad hoc)* what about Paris?

*(Fersen and Marie consider this.)*

Paris yes Paris Is that.
Isn't that a good *idea*?
MARIE: Well it's something.
LOUIS: You think it's a solution?
MARIE: Try it.

*(Beat.)*

LOUIS *(Panic attack)*: OK.

*(He won't leave.)*

*(Sickly smile)* But it's a
Really good idea right?
MARIE *(Tense smile)*: Unless you want to accede to their reforms.
LOUIS *(Bites his nails)*: Right. No //
MARIE: Don't bite your nails.
LOUIS: I //
MARIE *(Hurrying him along)*: Better get going //
FERSEN *(Supportive)*: Bye!

[STOP]

LOUIS: You // don't think
MARIE *(Hysterical, jarring)*: JUST-DO-IT-ALREADY!!

*(Louis exits abruptly; Marie throws herself down on the divan,
exhales.
A long recuperative silence; pace slows considerably, it's more
intimate. Fersen looks over at her.)*

FERSEN: I read it you know.

MARIE: What.

FERSEN: Your "autobiography."

MARIE: (Oh god.)

FERSEN *(Not titillated; ironic)*: You've been very naughty.

MARIE: Yes but I've expiated my sins evidently.

*(Pause.)*

I can't believe what's happening Axel
people are walking around *sans culottes*
they're burning us in effigy
it's gone haywire.

FERSEN: The whole thing will quash itself.
Tempers flare and then they die out and things go back to
normal. *(Beat)* It's just a lot of noise.

*(Pause.)*

MARIE: I've been having nightmares
Last night I was eaten by a pack of wolves . . .

*(She breaks down all at once. He goes to her.)*

*(Very vulnerable)* I'm sorry
It's
it's just that my *son* is really sick? everything
is coming at me all at once //

FERSEN: It's a lot of // pressure

MARIE: I feel like I'm inside a gyroscope All that—spinning
you know And the axis and—no gravity to hold it in place.

*(Beat.)*

FERSEN: What happened to my butterfly queen?

49

MARIE *(Wipes her tears)*: Oh god She's back in the chrysalis //

FERSEN: No //

MARIE *(Playing)*: *Yes* reverting to her caterpillar state and all ready to crawl back to Austria for a linzer tart.

FERSEN *(Small laugh)*: Give me a break //

MARIE: I'm serious.

FERSEN: You've never *crawled* in your life.

MARIE *(Some of the old impudence, but it's endearing)*: Well that's true.

*(They laugh; it subsides. Pause. Quiet. Marie is increasingly fearful again.)*

*(A fearful confession)* This man? he accosted me at the assembly, he was
in all black A peasant probably.
It was very ominous.
His face was like a bullet:
And he said to me:
"You think *this* is bad? *this* is just a preamble
to your suffering."

*(Beat; she snaps out of it. She artifices a queenly smile. She offers him chocolates from a box.)*

Dark or light?

FERSEN: They're just trying to scare you.

MARIE: Je ne sais pas.

FERSEN *(Rueful)*: People will do anything to get power.

## 8.

*Marie's boudoir, Petit Trianon.*
*Marie is pacing frantically. Lamballe is looking after the Dauphin.*

MARIE: And I've lost all my friends, so much for my "coterie"—
LAMBALLE: (I feel like I'm not getting much // credit)
MARIE *(Not hearing her)*: Ignominious pricks They pack off and
    leave without so much as a word //
LAMBALLE: Who //
MARIE: The Polignacs, Count of Artois INGRATES //
DAUPHIN: Maman? //
MARIE *(Snaps)*: Laissez-moi //
LAMBALLE: (I'll watch him) //
MARIE: (No-stay-here-with-me-I'm-freakin-out) //
LAMBALLE: I'll get you a glass of water //
MARIE: I'M-NOT-THIRSTY.

*(Pause.)*

LAMBALLE *(Starting to lose patience)*: Please calm down //
MARIE: I'm not stupid I know what's happening—there's riots all over the city Lamballe— Where is Louis he was supposed to be here yesterday I haven't heard a thing //
LAMBALLE: Where'd he go //
MARIE: Paris I—DON'T YOU LISTEN TO ANYTHING I SAY he dispatched troops weeks ago //
LAMBALLE: Maybe he got // delayed
MARIE: That should've put an end to it //
LAMBALLE: He's probably //
MARIE: "Probably" I don't tarry in probabilities Thérèse I need to know what's happening //
LAMBALLE *(Snaps, shouts at her)*: I DON'T KNOW WHAT TO SAY.

*(Marie's chastened. She sighs, penitent.)*

MARIE: I know I'm being totally crazy right now I know that. And I know there's something I should be doing, to rectify all this but I don't know what it is. Do you know? What is it?
LAMBALLE: Some things are out of your control.
MARIE *(Snaps)*: *Well that's not good enough.*
LAMBALLE: WELL THAT'S WHAT I HAVE TO OFFER YOU!

*(Pause.)*

MARIE: I'm *trying*. I *am*. but maybe there's something I don't see, I don't know some kind of blind spot? and I can't seem to overcome it?

*(Beat.)*

LAMBALLE *(Oddly direct)*: Maybe you're right.

MARIE: I don't know what to do.

LAMBALLE *(More gingerly)*: You're grieving.

You lost a child.

He only just died.

MARIE *(Very tiny)*: *But I should be responsible.*

LAMBALLE: You're a queen. You're not exempt from misfortune.

MARIE: Maybe I neglect them

I don't know my mother neglected me To me it's normal.

*(Pause.)*

Do you know when I got to Versailles Mother spied on me She did. *(Beat)* Spied on me and punished and exhorted me and never raised me.

*(She's submerged in a mental fog.)*

Sometimes I feel like . . . I'm not even a . . . person . . .

*(Pause; then demurring.)*

Do you ever feel that way?

*(A pause as Lamballe attempts to hide her own deeply uncomfortable recognition.)*

LAMBALLE *(Bluntly)*: No.

MARIE: I'm sure I'm just upset. And you're right. It should all be fine.

*(A weird silence.*
*Louis enters. He's wearing the tricolor cockade in his hat; we*
*instantly know something's deeply wrong.)*

What happened?

LOUIS: I had to send them back.

MARIE *(Incredulous)*: What is that.

*(He doesn't answer.)*

What IS that?

*(She rips the cockade from his hat.)*

*(Rising slowly)* Are you crazy.

LOUIS: There was a huge mob. They wanted—I don't know, *gunpowder?*

MARIE: *Gun*powder? What // are you

LOUIS: They came from the Invalides,

MARIE: What mob? Where? Where // are you

LOUIS: They broke in there, they-they got all these *guns* and um //

MARIE: WHAT MOB?

LOUIS: The Bastille—there was a whole—they killed all these people //

MARIE: WHO? //

LOUIS: They dragged the governor into the streets, they they stabbed him, they s-*sawed* off his head. And. It's . . . I don't know, there's . . . a new city *government* . . . ?

*(Marie reacts. Lamballe covers her mouth.)*

*(Referring to the cockade)* I had to.

[STOP]

MARIE: Thérèse you should go //
LOUIS *(A boy)*: I'm // scared.
MARIE *(Taking the Dauphin)*: I'll take him LEAVE //
LAMBALLE: But
  Will you be // all right?
MARIE: YES JUST GO.

*(Lamballe is paralyzed.)*

*(Increasingly worried)* LEAVE.
LAMBALLE: But I
  I can't // just
MARIE: YES YOU CAN JUST *LEAVE!*

*(Lamballe exits. The lights shift. A riot.)*

TITLE: A MOB OF THOUSANDS GATHERS IN PARIS AND
MARCHES ON VERSAILLES

TITLE: THEY DISCOVER A GATE TO THE PALACE IS UNLOCKED

TITLE: THEY STORM THE PALACE AND SEARCH FOR THE QUEEN

TITLE: A RIOT

## 9.

*Versailles. It's wrecked.*
*Marie is holding suitcases. Louis has just entered the room. They're*
*looking away from each other. A tableau.*
*Silence.*

MARIE: I had them pack our things.
LOUIS: We can't leave.

  *(She turns to him.)*

MARIE: Everyone's escaped but *us //*
LOUIS: But I think it might be worse
    If we tried to escape don't you think?
MARIE *(Flabbergasted)*: HOW?

HOW can it be WORSE?

They threatened to roast me on a *spit*.

LOUIS: Don't be outré.

MARIE: OUTRÉ??!

They want to EAT me //

LOUIS: No //

MARIE: Literally: Yes! they were saying things like "I want the thigh meat! I want the leg!" I had to get out on the balcony.

LOUIS: What did you say?

MARIE: I feel your pain (and then I curtsied).

LOUIS: *That's* convincing.

MARIE: *Well* it was the best I could muster //

LOUIS *(Mollifying)*: Of // course

MARIE: And you don't KNOW Louis They still LIKE you To them I'm just some bitch from Austria who gives everyone *blowjobs* //

LOUIS: Please keep your comportment //

MARIE: It's true //

LOUIS: You're still // a queen

MARIE: And I'm *keeping* my comportment Do you know what I was doing as they waved their hatchets at me and threw rocks?

*(She waves a queen-like wave and smiles a frozen smile.)*

LOUIS *(Approbation)*: That's *very* regal.

*(She gives him a look.)*

*What?*

*(She's thinking "this is really my life, oh god.")*

DAVID ADJMI

MARIE: Play with your clocks I'm going back to Austria.

*(She grabs the suitcases.)*

LOUIS: Wait a minute let's just think this through.
MARIE: No! No more indecision!
LOUIS: I CAN'T JUST LEAVE
    I HAVE A RESPONSIBILITY.

*(She eyeballs him.)*

MARIE: You have a *responsibility*.
    To *me*.
LOUIS: I can't just abandon everything.

*(Marie looks at him, helplessly.)*

MARIE: Then stay.

*(She picks up the suitcases.)*

LOUIS: You're leaving?
MARIE: Yes.

*(Pause.)*

LOUIS: You're going to leave me?

*(Short pause.)*

MARIE *(Not flip)*: It's been nice Louis.
    But I've never been in love with you.
    And I won't be undone by you. Sorry.

*(Pause.)*

LOUIS: Oh.

*(Pause.)*

MARIE *(Now feels awful)*: You're not coming?
LOUIS: I just
　　I
　　I need to think.

*(Marie holds her suitcases, looking at him.*
*She's about to walk out.*
*Louis is completely rudderless.*
*Fuck.*
*She can't do it.*
*She puts the suitcases down.*
*Louis buries his head in her breast and weeps.)*

# 10.

*A Revolutionary appears, accosts Marie.*

REVOLUTIONARY: Necklace:

*(She removes her necklace with difficulty; hands it to him.)*

Rings:

*(She reluctantly removes her rings.)*

MARIE: Who will draw my bath.
REVOLUTIONARY: Bracelets:
MARIE: I'm tired.
REVOLUTIONARY: Hairpiece:

MARIE: You don't need to take that.

*(He looks up at her.)*

*(A bitch)* I don't see why I should give you anything—

*(He rips it off her head, she screams.)*

[STOP]

Where are my servants.
REVOLUTIONARY: Gone.
MARIE: Who will draw my bath.
REVOLUTIONARY: You will not bathe
You have been stripped of the privilege.
MARIE: I feel ill:
where // is
REVOLUTIONARY: Shh //
MARIE *(Rage)*: DON'T SHUSH ME—

*(He slaps her. Hard.)*

REVOLUTIONARY *(Quiet but in her face)*: You know what I see
when I look at you?
Bracelets:
Silk:
A hairdo.

[STOP]

MARIE *(Humiliated but trying to stay regal)*: This is all a bit *de trop* don't you think?

*(He grabs her by the throat.)*

REVOLUTIONARY *(Looking through her)*: You don't understand.
It's not the same.
It's not the same
Anymore.

*(She nods, slowly, acquiescent, a harrowing understanding.)*

# ACT TWO

## 1.

Title: 1791

*The Tuileries.*
*Marie is doing needlepoint.*
*The Dauphin is bored.*

MARIE: Go play in the gardens There's mazes.
DAUPHIN: I want to see Paris.
MARIE: You can get lost.
DAUPHIN: I don't want to play in the gardens.
MARIE: You're being very naughty.
DAUPHIN (*Insulted*): I'm *not* naughty.
MARIE: You can't see Paris now.
DAUPHIN: Why?
MARIE: Because we're in the Tuileries, isn't it lovely?

*(Beat.)*

DAUPHIN: Which arrondissement are we in?
MARIE: Go off and play,
DAUPHIN: I don't *like* the Tuileries //
MARIE: Now //
DAUPHIN *(Tantrum)*: I DON'T WANT TO PLAY IN THE
GARDENS!

[STOP]

*(He looks at her: an impasse.*
*Louis enters.)*

LOUIS: Smashing game of billiards //
MARIE: (We have to talk) //
LOUIS *(Referring to her handiwork)*: Needlepoint?
MARIE: Louis:
LOUIS: What is it, a jug?
MARIE: We have to get out of here.
LOUIS: What do you think I'd been *planning* //
MARIE: Shh put this on.

*(She produces a farmer's outfit.)*

LOUIS: What is it.
MARIE: A disguise.
LOUIS: Where'd you get that.
MARIE: We're going to Varennes.
LOUIS: What *is* this?!
MARIE *(Hurriedly applying his fake mustache)*: We're farmers.

*(She puts on her farmer costume.)*

It's all arranged, General Bouillé will meet us there and we'll be safe, there's an army, and we can escape at the border.

*(She looks at him, fixes his hat; they look crazy.)*

There:
LOUIS: How do I look?

*(Beat.)*

MARIE *(Perfunctory)*: Yeah It looks good Come on—

2.

*The carriage.*
*On the way to Varennes.*

MARIE: We've been riding forever,
LOUIS: We're almost there,
MARIE: It's cramped, I need to stretch.
DAUPHIN: I have to pee.
LOUIS: Can you hold it?
DAUPHIN: I think so //
MARIE: Now where are we?
LOUIS: Sainte-Ménehould //
MARIE: (Ugh my back) //
LOUIS: We're almost there,
DAUPHIN: I can't hold it!
LOUIS: Let's not stop till we get to Varennes.

MARIE: "Stop the carriage" (It'll just be for a second) //
LOUIS: We're almost there.


*(It stops.)*


MARIE *(To the Dauphin)*: Go and pee darling //
LOUIS: *Marie—*


*(They dismount the carriage. The Dauphin runs off. Marie stretches. Louis takes a brief survey of the landscape.)*


Why is it like this?
MARIE: Like what?
LOUIS *(Making a face)*: Rocks and things.
MARIE: It's called nature.
LOUIS: I know what nature is.
MARIE: You've led a very protected existence
    This is real life.
LOUIS: I know what real life is I'm not saying that,
MARIE: When I lived in Austria // I
LOUIS: "The Danube, the shepherds" //
MARIE: All *right* You don't have to be derisory I'm just saying //
LOUIS: Je m'en fiche.
MARIE: (Don't be *crude*)
LOUIS: (I learned how to curse)
MARIE *(Brushing it off)*: You're crabby.
    *(She sits on the ground)*
    Oh look a little earthworm. You know you can chop these
    up into a million pieces They're indestructible. I always
    liked nature. *(She looks around)* Look darling there's a
    windmill. It's like the one I had built at le Hameau.
LOUIS: There's not many variations on windmills.
MARIE: What do they do, do you think.

LOUIS: Windmills?
  *(He shrugs)*
  They're ornamental.
MARIE: Don't they have a function?
LOUIS: Beauty's a function.

*(Marie laughs.)*

MARIE: You're so shallow.

*(Marie laughs.)*

LOUIS: *I'm* shallow?
MARIE: There's more to life than glittery things dear //
LOUIS *(Umbrage)*: Yes I *know* that //
MARIE *(Teasingly)*: You're just so incredibly cosseted,
LOUIS: I can hardly accept that sort of indictment from the likes // of you
MARIE *(Sharp turn)*: I CUT BACK I TOLD YOU THAT A MILLION TIMES!

*(A tense pause.)*

LOUIS *(Looks away)*: Anyway the damage is done.

*(Beat.)*

MARIE: "Damage."

*(He doesn't answer.)*

Well that was below the belt Thanks.

*(After a long pause the Dauphin enters.)*

DAUPHIN: Daddy I'm hungry.
LOUIS: We're nearly there Be patient,
MARIE: Did you pee.

*(The Dauphin nods.)*

LOUIS *(To Marie)*: Shall we?
MARIE *(Still smarting)*: My back's killing me Help me up.

*(They're about to get back in the carriage. Marie spies something in the distance.)*

Oh wait there's someone //
LOUIS: *Let's go, // quickly*
MARIE: "Excusez-moi" //
LOUIS: (What are you doing—)
MARIE: (I want to ask them something) "Helloo?"

*(Mr. Sauce, the shopkeeper, enters with his wife.)*

MR. SAUCE: Hi.
MARIE: Bonjour. Or. I mean "hi"—well I don't know but //
MRS. SAUCE: Hi //
MARIE: (Yes hi) Would you mind resolving an argument between my husband and me, we were wondering: What do windmills do Are they just decorative or do they have a function? Or:

*(Beat.)*

MR. SAUCE: Windmills.
MARIE: Yes.

*(Beat.)*

MRS. SAUCE: Aren'tcha farmers?

LOUIS *(Takes her by the arm)*: She's just // kidding

MARIE *(Impromptu, pulls away)*: We are farmers but you see we're very new farmers We're sort of neophytes and we don't know all the technicalities.

*(Mr. Sauce and Mrs. Sauce exchange looks.)*

MR. SAUCE: You grind things.

*(Beat.)*

MARIE: What?

MRS. SAUCE: *Windmills.*

MARIE: Oh.

MR. SAUCE: You grind things.

MARIE: Oh So they *do* have a function //

LOUIS *(Tries to get Marie in the carriage)*: Well you were right That solves // that OK bye

MARIE *(Magnetized to them)*: Do you live around here? HOLD ON A SECOND (What an interesting frock) //

*(Marie feels her frock.)*

MRS. SAUCE: Thank // you

MARIE: If you don't mind my asking are you in a business of some kind? Or //

MR. SAUCE: We're shopkeepers //

MARIE *(Delighted)*: *Shop*keepers! *R*eally!

MR. SAUCE: We're right down that road.

MARIE *(Takes them by the arm)*: And what does that involve? *(Earnest)*
I mean—like What sort of life is it?
Is it
Spiritually nourishing?

*(They look at her.)*

I mean . . . do you feel like a . . . real . . . *person?*
MR. SAUCE *(Suspicious; to Louis)*: You look familiar //
DAUPHIN: Maman I'm *hun*gry,
MR. SAUCE: Where've I seen you?

*(He and Mrs. Sauce exchange a look.)*

LOUIS: We *really should* be going. Darling?

*(Louis extends his hand to her. Mrs. Sauce grabs her arm.)*

MR. SAUCE *(Stalling)*: I'm Sauce and that's Mrs. Sauce.

*(Marie is a little unnerved.)*

MARIE: Hi.
MRS. SAUCE: Hi.

*(Lots of smiling.)*

MARIE: Well: it was *so* lovely to meet you
    I'm sure // we'll
DAUPHIN: I'm hungry!
MRS. SAUCE: Awwwww who's this sweet thing.
    "He-llo"
    "He-llo"

*(Sauce approaches the Dauphin.)*

MR. SAUCE: You hungry, Little Man?
DAUPHIN: We're going to Varennes.
MR. SAUCE: Varennes That's pretty far.

MRS. SAUCE: It's getting dark come spend the night chez nous.

LOUIS: No That's OK.

MR. SAUCE: You can't let your boy go hungry,
  *(Using a cutesy voice)* "Do you like potatoes?" //

DAUPHIN *(Shy)*: I like meat //

MR. SAUCE *(Pinches his cheeks)*: Awwww //

DAUPHIN: Ow!

MR. SAUCE: We have a room above the shop.

MRS. SAUCE: We can teach you about shopkeeping.

MR. SAUCE: You can have a nice sleep rest your little toesies.

*(Mr. Sauce grabs the Dauphin, it's somewhat violent, clutches him. A terrifying pause.)*

DAUPHIN *(Tiny, scared)*: Maman?

*(Pause.)*

MR. SAUCE: I'll take your luggage.

## 3.

*They remove their disguises.*
*They are back at the Tuileries.*
*Marie's hair has turned white.*

LOUIS: "Windmills."

MARIE: At least we got to see a shop.

LOUIS: Now what.

MARIE: There's sentinels everywhere; there's men watching me
undress, watching me sleep. It's much worse //

DAUPHIN: I want to go to Paris //

MARIE: (Mummy has a migraine darling) *Louis please do some-*
*thing,* I cannot live in a prison //

LOUIS: We're alive aren't we.

MARIE: Barely,

LOUIS: I'm trying to think //

MARIE: You have to act not think They'll kill us in our // sleep

*(A Revolutionary edges in and listens openly.)*

LOUIS: We have to b—

*(He stops—looks up at the Revolutionary.)*

*(Smiling tautly)* Hello.
REVOLUTIONARY 2: Hi.

*(Beat.)*

LOUIS: We're, uh: trying to have a *private* conversation?
REVOLUTIONARY 2: That's
    not allowed.
MARIE *(Taut smile)*: What do you mean it's not allowed //
REVOLUTIONARY 2: You may only converse with one another in
    the presence of guards.
MARIE: Really, why's that?
REVOLUTIONARY 2: Now that you've run away you're consid-
    ered émigrés.
LOUIS: What?
REVOLUTIONARY 2: Enemies of the state.

*(Pause.)*

MARIE: I see.
REVOLUTIONARY 2 *(Fake sheepish smile)*: Sorry.
MARIE: So: forgive me I'm a bit dense Let me recap:
    we *run* the state: but we're *enemies* of the state.
REVOLUTIONARY 2: Yes.

*(Beat.)*

MARIE: Well that makes a ton of // sense.

REVOLUTIONARY 2: There's a revolution //

MARIE: A *revolution fine* but can't we have a private
Conversation //

REVOLUTIONARY 2: No.

[STOP]

MARIE: Well: I realize we're prisoners and everything but we're
going to need *some* privacy. And that's just how it *is*.

REVOLUTIONARY 2: No.

*(Marie looks at him, flaring insolence.)*

MARIE: "No"

*(The Revolutionary chuckles, looks away.)*

*(Temper flaring)* I've made my life public for *your* delecta-
tion and *your* scrutiny and you won't allow *me* a private
conversation with my own *husband*?

REVOLUTIONARY 2: No.

MARIE: That's kind of you, this "revolution" is very civilized.

REVOLUTIONARY 2: Civilization's a luxury we can't afford.

MARIE: What do we get in its stead? lopped heads and fresh-
cut THROATS?

LOUIS: Marie:

MARIE *(To Louis)*: NO, I'M SORRY, MY HAIR'S TURNED
*WHITE*!

REVOLUTIONARY 2 *(Quoting)*: "Terror without virtue is disastrous
and virtue without terror is impossible" //

MARIE *(Covering her face in frustration)*: Whatever //

DAUPHIN: I'm hungry //

REVOLUTIONARY 2: We've written a constitution // "Liberté

MARIE: (Marvelous) //

REVOLUTIONARY 2: Égalité // Fraternité"

MARIE *(Indignation)*: Yeah yeah stop blathering My son wants a *flan* or something can't we get a decent *meal?* //

REVOLUTIONARY 2: A decent *meal* //

MARIE: *Yes* a decent *meal* We're very *hungry* //

REVOLUTIONARY 2: I could starve you to death if I wanted.

MARIE: *Excuse* // me

REVOLUTIONARY 2: I could snap your necks and I'd get a standing ovation.

MARIE: *What.*

*(She lifts her hand to strike him, Louis stops her.)*

LOUIS: She's tired.

*(She shakes Louis off; stares the Revolutionary down.)*

MARIE *(Frightened but hiding it)*: You're not some acolyte of enlightenment you know.

You're very young and you don't know much of anything.

REVOLUTIONARY 2: And you're very *old.*

MARIE: I'm thirty-seven // It's

REVOLUTIONARY 2: OLDER.

MARIE: What are you talking about.

REVOLUTIONARY 2: The *Ancien Régime.*

MARIE: You don't make any sense //

REVOLUTIONARY 2: Maybe the sense can be knocked into your head once we've sliced it off your neck.

*(He's scared her.)*

LOUIS: Don't speak to my wife like that.

REVOLUTIONARY 2: Don't tell me how to speak
As if I'm to have reverence for you.

*(The Revolutionary spits in Louis's face.)*

LOUIS: I'm still your king.

REVOLUTIONARY 2: No you are shit; "And you will die so France can live."

*(Pause; Louis wipes off the spit.)*

LOUIS: I don't see it as so mutually exclusive.

REVOLUTIONARY 2: That's not me It's Robespierre,

MARIE: Oh // god

LOUIS: That *dandy?*

REVOLUTIONARY 2: He's not a dandy and his panegyrics on the system of revolutionary government and his praise of virtue // show

MARIE: "Virtue" oh SHUT UP!

REVOLUTIONARY 2: how the system // of

MARIE: Can't he just have a nice little provincial practice as a LAWYER?

*(No response.)*

Well. Good for him. OK then.

*(The Revolutionary doesn't leave.)*

Bye.

*(He doesn't leave.)*

*(To Louis; bitter sarcasm)* He's *very* charming.

LOUIS: He spat in my face.

MARIE *(Terribly cutting)*: Yes but there's a way of spitting in someone's face and being charming at the same time:

*(Beat.)*

it's a *talent.*
Like *juggling.*

*(She smiles a fake smile at the Revolutionary who smiles back, equally fake.)*

# 4.

*The Tuileries.*
*Marie—with a tin of biscuits—is working feverishly on some kind*
*of makeshift espionage.*

LOUIS: Billiards?
MARIE *(Distracted)*: No.
LOUIS: What's that?
MARIE: Cipher.
LOUIS *(Perked up)*: What do you mean Like a *code*? //
MARIE: Shh, they'll hear—
LOUIS: In a box of *biscuits*? //
MARIE: *Can it.*
LOUIS: Since when do you know how to write in *cipher* //
MARIE *(Feverish)*: (I'm-not-dying-in-the-fuckin-tuileries-that's-
    for-fuckin-certain-we're-getting-the-*fuck*-out-of-here!) //

LOUIS: What's going on //

MARIE: (Go play billiards) //

LOUIS *(Snooping in the box)*: Are there any biscuits left? //

MARIE *(Wrests box, slaps hand)*: *Louis!* //

LOUIS: (Or.) //

MARIE *(Stage whisper)*: Did you know that eight hundred men from Marseille have arrived and the deputies of the Jacobin clubs?

LOUIS: And?

MARIE: It's a pretty blunt gesture don't you think They're out to destroy us, openly, there's no pretense anymore, *at all*.

LOUIS: Where'd you hear this?

MARIE: Fersen.

LOUIS: He's *alive*?

MARIE: We've been writing each other.

LOUIS: *That's dangerous //*

MARIE: SHHH!

LOUIS: That's what you've been sewing into hat linings? //

MARIE *(Gleeful)*: (And I do it with pinpricks as well It's a kind of code)

LOUIS *(Delighted)*: *No!*

MARIE *(Looks around, nervous)*: *You think they saw me?*

LOUIS: You're ingenious //

MARIE: (I can't tell if I'm being paranoid or judicious.)

LOUIS: Why didn't you tell me?

MARIE: Because you're *apathetic* //

LOUIS: I'M NOT APATHETIC //

MARIE *(Whisper)*: *Shut up!*

*(We hear the faint sound of church bells gonging.)*

LOUIS: I hate when you say that, I'm just *thinking*: biding my *options* We don't want to be feckless //

MARIE: I think it's a bit late for "feckless."

*(Louis hears the bells. Puzzled, turns to Marie.)*

LOUIS: What's going on?

*(Marie reacts.)*

MARIE: *Oh my god . . .*
LOUIS: What.
MARIE: You're not gonna believe it: Fersen told the Duke of
Brunswick about us And he sent this letter to the Jacobins
saying that if they do even the smallest violence to us the
whole city of Paris will be *destroyed*!
LOUIS: So:
MARIE: Don't you see? we're getting out of here.
LOUIS: We are?
MARIE: You think they'd let it escalate to that? We're getting
out of here!

*(Beat.*
*They do a little dance of excitement. The Royalist walks in on*
*them.)*

ROYALIST: Sire //
LOUIS *(Caught dancing)*: Yes what is it.
ROYALIST: I'm. sorry to disrupt // your
LOUIS: That's quite all right.
ROYALIST: I. Have some unfortunate news
I'm afraid //
MARIE *(Claps her hands together with ersatz delight)*: Ooh a change
of pace how tonic.
LOUIS: What's the matter?
ROYALIST: There's riots everywhere; prisons are being opened
everyone's getting hacked to pieces it's a nightmare.

*(Pause.)*

LOUIS: Oh.

*(Pause.)*

ROYALIST: They're trying to frighten the royalists evidently.

LOUIS: Are we safe?

ROYALIST: Word is they're going to converge on the Tuileries next.

*(Marie smiles.)*

MARIE *(Flirtatious good humor)*: But that can't happen.

ROYALIST *(To Louis)*: I fear they'll kill you if you // stay

MARIE *(Total denial)*: (No darling it's a mistake of some kind) You must have some Misinformation.

ROYALIST: I'm afraid not Your // Majesty

MARIE *(Cracking somewhat)*: *You listen to me:*
The Duke of Brunswick has *vowed* to protect us Do you understand the *magnitude* of the consequences if his orders are breeched?

LOUIS *(To Marie, tentative)*: Maybe it backfired.

ROYALIST: Forgive me. But. I must ask you both to take refuge on the assembly.

*(Marie looks up.)*

MARIE: The *assembly.*

*(She laughs.)*

ROYALIST *(Discomfited by her)*: They're meeting at the old riding grounds //

MARIE: That would be the same assembly that took up residence on our tennis courts and wants us DEAD *That* assembly?

ROYALIST: I know how it must // sound

MARIE: And they're to be our *refuge.*

ROYALIST: It's for your own good Your // Majesty

MARIE *(Breaking comportment)*: *My* own good?

Are you *joking*?

ROYALIST: It is your best // hope

MARIE: Are you *kidding*?

LOUIS *(To Marie)*: It does seem dire //

MARIE *(Fillip of rage)*: HE'S LYING.

LOUIS: You heard what he said They'll kill us if we stay.

*(Beat.)*

MARIE *(Regains composure)*: Then they'll have to kill me here.

LOUIS: I think we should listen to him.

MARIE: I'm going to take a nap.

LOUIS *(Grabs her arm as she leaves)*: Wait a // minute I

MARIE: YOU SHUT UP if it weren't for you we wouldn't even be here in the first place (get off me) //

LOUIS: But we have // to

MARIE *(Breaks free)*: *No*, you've made all the wrong choices for us, *unfailingly*, *every* time, I won't budge!

LOUIS *(Reaching for her)*: I //

MARIE: Fuck off No You can nail me to the WALLS FIRST.

*(The sound of glass shattering.)*

TITLE: THE TUILERIES IS INVADED

TITLE: SIX HUNDRED PEOPLE ARE SLAUGHTERED

TITLE: THE ROYAL FAMILY IS ESCORTED TO THE ASSEMBLY

TITLE: THE MOB DESCENDS UPON THE ASSEMBLY

TITLE: DEMANDING THE DEPOSITION OF THE KING

TITLE: AND CUSTODY OF THE ROYAL FAMILY

## 5.

*The sound of rioting outside.*
*The royal family is crowded in a tiny room, sitting in terror.*
*It's hot.*
*Marie paces.*
*Long silence.*

MARIE: I feel faint.

   *(Beat.)*

   I feel faint.
LOUIS: Be still.
MARIE: It's sweltering and somebody stole my purse on the way.
DAUPHIN: I want to take a bath.

MARIE: This is torture.

*(She covers her ears. Long pause.)*

Why don't they kill us What are they waiting for.
LOUIS: They won't kill us.
MARIE: Won't they.
LOUIS: Listen to me: we'll get out of this.

*(Marie says nothing.)*

I know what you think of me
But I promise you
I'll get us out of this.

*(Marie says nothing.)*

Look at me.
MARIE: What.

*(Louis sings a serenade to her—odd, sweet, funny—to the sounds of fighting, cannon fire, battle cries in the background.)*

LOUIS:

Un rêve jolie t'attend
Quand le sommeil t'en prend

Beaux rêves
Venez à mon bébé
Beaux rêves
Venez à mon bébé

La nuit approche, le jour finit
Endors-toi, petit chéri

Beaux rêves
Venez à mon bébé
Beaux rêves
Venez à mon bébé . . .

*(Louis looks at her.)*

MARIE: That was off-key.

*(A beat. He breaks into laughter.*
*They all break into laughter.*
*The sounds of bullets and bloodshed over their laughter.)*

# 6.

*A holding cell. Two Guards watch over Marie and the Dauphin.*

MARIE: Where is he.

*(No answer.)*

Where is my husband.

DAUPHIN: Maman //

MARIE *(To Guards)*: WHY WON'T YOU TELL ME ANY-
THING!

*(Long awful silence.)*

*"Oh really that's so interesting."*

DAUPHIN *(Softly, sad, apologetic)*: (Maman, I do want to play in
the gardens.)

*(Pause.)*

MARIE *(Ignoring the Dauphin, to the Guard)*: LOOK is he alive, dead, what.

*(No answer.)*

DAUPHIN *(Tugging at her sleeve)*: Maman?

*(Beat.)*

Maman //
MARIE: *WHAT*:

*(Beat.)*

DAUPHIN *(Demurs; she's scary)*: I want to play in the gardens.
MARIE *(Strain)*: Sweetheart
   You can't play in the gardens
   Now.

*(Pause.)*

DAUPHIN *(Tears; quiet)*: I want to play in the // gardens
MARIE: DID YOU HEAR WHAT I SAID
   YOU CAN'T PLAY IN THE GARDENS.

*(Pause.)*

DAUPHIN: Why?
MARIE: Because there's no gardens anymore.
DAUPHIN: Why //
MARIE: BECAUSE WE'RE PRISONERS.

*(She falls apart; it's too much. The Dauphin grabs onto her dress, frightened.)*

DAUPHIN: Don't cry.

*(She doesn't answer.)*

Don't //
MARIE: Will you get: OFF ME.

*(She pushes him away from her, very violent.
Immediately she regrets this, realizes what she's done.
A Guard picks up the Dauphin.)*

GUARD *(Whispers to the other Guard)*: Portez-le à l'autre salle.

*(He carries off the Dauphin.)*

MARIE: What are you doing
Where are you going *I didn't mean that.*
WHAT ARE YOU DOING WITH HIM, THAT'S MY SON!
*(Shaking, hysterical)*
C-c-c-come back
Where are
Wh-wh-wh
Wh

*(Marie weeps and weeps. The lights darken.
The sounds of water dripping.
Underground, the Conciergerie. A week or so later, but seamless.
From now through the end of the play the scenes should begin
bleeding together. We should lose the sense of any clear demarca-
tion between the beginnings and endings of scenes.
The Sheep appears.)*

SHEEP: Comment allez-vous.

MARIE: Sheep?

SHEEP: Comment allez-vous Marie.

MARIE: What's happening to me?

SHEEP: I'm so sorry.

MARIE: I haven't seen you since that day, in the fields, at Trianon.

SHEEP: Yes, it's been a while.

MARIE: I don't even know what's become of Versailles.

SHEEP: Be careful Marie.

MARIE: Of what?

SHEEP *(Softly)*: Don't go mad.

MARIE: I WON'T! My mother told me never to fear death so I'm very resolute.

SHEEP: Your hand is shaking.

MARIE: They separated the Dauphin from me, out of spite, they put him in a cell beneath me, I could hear him crying for me. Then they moved me underground—but I don't know where I am . . .

SHEEP: The Conciergerie.

MARIE: But they left my son in the Temple, do you know what's happened to him?

SHEEP: No I'm just a sheep.

*(She looks at him. She laughs.)*

MARIE: Oh my god This is a comedy.

SHEEP: Baaa.

MARIE *(Wipes her eyes)*: Well it's better than nothing.

[STOP]

Do you know I begged them to let him stay? *Begged* them. But the minister laughed at me, "You Austrian whore why do you feign love for this bastard"—it's so funny I'm an AUSTRIAN whore I love the qualifiers—as if AUS-TRIAN makes me somehow more lurid Like I'm MORE whorish because I'm Austrian.

[STOP]

(They were happy to have me when I was a queen) I'M STILL A FUCKING QUEEN!!

*(Pause; she's embarrassed, tries to retract.)*

*(Forcing hope)* The Austrian army has crossed the border of France They're forty leagues from Paris, surely they will come for me. I'm still royal there. They have to come for me. Don't they?

SHEEP: You look exhausted.

MARIE: I can't get any rest; I close my eyes and just lie there.

SHEEP: It helps to count sheep.

*(She looks at him.)*

MARIE: One.

*(Beat.)*

SHEEP: Maybe it's better to count backwards //

MARIE: Backwards from one? //

SHEEP: Is this too abstract //

MARIE: Yes and you know I'm not good at abstract thinking; that's what Countess Brandeis used to say.

SHEEP: You're better at concrete thinking? //

MARIE: The truth is I HATE thinking! I do, I have problems focusing—you know what I miss, I miss gambling,

I miss my friends. I miss my little biscuit and espresso in the morning. *(Beat)* You must think I'm acting all sorry for myself.

SHEEP: No.

MARIE: You're very understanding; Animals are so absolving.

SHEEP: Thank you.

MARIE: I miss nature.

*(A beat; the Sheep moves closer to her; very gingerly.)*

SHEEP: Rousseau believed in the primacy of human nature.

*(Marie looks at him.)*

MARIE: Did he?

SHEEP: That people are good but society is a corrupting force.

*(Pause.)*

MARIE: Do you believe that?

*(Beat.)*

SHEEP: What do *you* believe?

*(Pause.)*

MARIE *(To herself; a discovery)*: I don't know.

*(The Sheep takes a step toward her.)*

SHEEP: You should have read Rousseau //
MARIE *(Echoing him)*: I should've read Rousseau Voltaire;
    I should have memorized the
    maxims of La Rochefoucauld.

SHEEP: "We always love those who admire us, but we do not always love those whom we admire."

MARIE *(Trying to memorize as he speaks it)*: Another:

SHEEP: "True love, however rare, is still more common than true friendship."

MARIE: Tell me more,

SHEEP: What about?

*(Beat.)*

MARIE *(Deeply sincere)*: Teach me.

[STOP]

SHEEP: Are you familiar with Newton's work in physics?

MARIE *(Freaking out)*: Who's he?

SHEEP *(Soft, gentle smile)*: Isaac Newton proved how natural events conform to underlying laws. This showed people like Voltaire that nature could be used as a model for human society.

MARIE: Voltaire wanted to come see me at court but I refused him Should I invite him back?

SHEEP: Too late for that.

*(Beat.)*

MARIE: Trianon's gone, that's right,

SHEEP: And he's dead.

MARIE: They hacked him up?

SHEEP: Natural causes.

MARIE: And who's Isaac Newman?

SHEEP: Isaac *Newton* believed in an intelligible order that under- lies all of nature //

MARIE: I agree with that.

*(The Sheep nods no.)*

I don't?

SHEEP: You believe in Absolute Monarchy.

MARIE: Well I'm the queen.

SHEEP: Monarchy has its roots in inequality.

MARIE: So:

SHEEP: Inequality is unnatural.

MARIE: What's the alternative?

*(A beat.)*

SHEEP: Democracy.

*(Beat. Marie laughs. The Sheep does not. Marie looks at him.)*

MARIE: No really.

SHEEP: Now you've insulted me.

MARIE *(Struggling)*: But common people can't take care of them*selves*. Democracy can't work.

SHEEP: Hierarchy cannot survive because it goes against the laws of nature //

MARIE: Yes and Democracy is godless rule.

SHEEP: Come now, you don't really believe in God.

MARIE: Sheep you're blasphemous.

SHEEP *(Gentle)*: The only god is Natural Law. Reason.

*(Long pause.)*

MARIE *(Totally rudderless)*: I don't know what to believe.

*(Pause.)*

SHEEP *(Hypnotic; an incantation)*: "Liberté, égalité, fraternité . . ."

MARIE (*Recoiling*): Perhaps I should've treated my subjects with greater consideration I've tried to amend that. But Common People can't take care of themselves, they can't make decisions, they aren't *sovereign* //

SHEEP (*Sudden virulent shift, an attack*): NO—*YOU* CAN'T TAKE CARE OF *YOUR*SELF! *YOU* CAN'T MAKE DECISIONS! *YOU* AREN'T SOVEREIGN!

(*Pause.*)

MARIE (*Grasping at straws*): I'm Queen of France.

(*The Sheep takes another step toward her.*)

(*Weakening, tired*) Just because something's modern doesn't make it true.

SHEEP: Use *Reason*.

MARIE (*Lost*): But I can't dispense with the past with history //

SHEEP: That's why you've become its victim.

And your own life was lost to you.

MARIE (*He's right*): I wish I could sleep.

SHEEP: Wake up.

[STOP]

(*The next section is to herself.*)

MARIE (*Sad, exhaustion*): What did you say? Count backwards?

SHEEP: Negative numbers: negative one, two //

MARIE: I was bad at math.

(*Long pause.*)

I feel so alone.

SHEEP *(Sweetly)*: Pet me.

*(A beat; she turns to him.)*

MARIE: Yes, I need to be close to someone.
SHEEP: "Ach du mein Kind."
MARIE: German, I haven't heard it since I was little, come
    Sheep //
SHEEP: Baa //
MARIE: Close to my heart.

*(As the Sheep approaches Marie, he sloughs off his sheepskin, revealing himself to be a wolf. This is magic, and it's terrifying. The wolf attacks her. We hear the loud growling, her cries, her screams.*
*Revolutionary 3 enters.)*

*(Disoriented)* How long have I been here.

*(The Revolutionary is preparing to shear her hair with a straight razor.)*

Where's my son?
REVOLUTIONARY 3: I have orders not to speak with the Widow
    Capet.
MARIE: "The: oh that's *me*?
    I see.

*(He starts to cut.)*

Not too short.

*(Pause.)*

I have fleas in my hair can I at least wash it?
*(He cuts)*
Guess not.
*(He cuts)*
"There once was a girl named Marie, whose head was infested with fleas—"
*(Laughter)*

[STOP]

When's my trial Can you tell me that.
REVOLUTIONARY 3: Two weeks.
MARIE: Thank you.

*(The waters of the Seine drip around them as he cuts her hair.)*

You can't understand it, but I was *born* to be a *queen*. It wasn't my *choosing*, I was born *into* it.

[STOP]

And I wasn't raised I was *built*: I was built to be this *thing*; and now they're killing me for it—but you'd be the same You'd make the same choices I did.
REVOLUTIONARY 3: And if you had my lot you'd choose the same as me.

*(Beat.)*

MARIE: What do you want
    From me
REVOLUTIONARY 3: We want to institute new ways of living.
MARIE *(Makes a connection)*: But I wanted the same *thing*,
REVOLUTIONARY 3: For *yourself* //

MARIE: That's //

REVOLUTIONARY 3: You think your bullshit pastoralism counts? While you paraded around in your *peasant* costume, *real* peasants were starving to death.

MARIE: Then I was wrong to do that! But is this how you exercise *virtue*? I don't *get* // it

REVOLUTIONARY 3: "Virtue without terror—

MARIE *(Exasperated)*: "is impossible" *yeah I* // *know*:

REVOLUTIONARY 3: We want equality //

MARIE: Right //

REVOLUTIONARY 3: Can you understand // that

MARIE: I don't have to "understand it" It's been jammed down // my throat

REVOLUTIONARY 3: And to get that we will *destroy you.*

*(He looks her in the eye.)*

Do you understand?
You will be *eradicated.*
*No one* will *remember* you.
And when we're done it'll be like *you never existed.*

*(He eyeballs her for a moment. Slowly, he makes his way behind her and resumes cutting.)*

MARIE *(Grasping at straws)*: But I had a right to be // queen

REVOLUTIONARY 3: Shut up.

MARIE: I ruled by divine—OW.
YOU CUT ME.

[STOP]

*(Sincerely pleading)* People's nature is *good,* isn't that what you believe, Rousseau? Isn't that what he says?

REVOLUTIONARY 3: You pervert Rousseau.

MARIE: Then tell me, what does he say?

> Really, I want to know.
>
> Teach me something, would you?
>
> *(Hysterical)* EDUCATE ME.

REVOLUTIONARY 3: I'm not supposed to speak to you.

MARIE: Why, you'll be arrested for treason?

REVOLUTIONARY 3: Head down.

MARIE *(Bitter)*: Oh that's *liberty* //

REVOLUTIONARY 3: *Quiet* //

MARIE: Not so short.

*(He cuts.)*

REVOLUTIONARY 3: Poor thing

> You act like everything's hurt you
>
> And everyone's used you
>
> And you're just some sweet sunburnt girl at the beach
>
> You won't look at reality.

MARIE: "Reality."

REVOLUTIONARY 3: Pity.

MARIE: The reality is you can't have a *nation* without a *king*.

REVOLUTIONARY 3: What about America?

MARIE *(Practically in tears)*: AMERICA:

> I'm so *sick* of hearing about AMERICA:
>
> America is a *doomed* experiment.
>
> Don't you see *this will weaken France to the point of extinction*?!

REVOLUTIONARY 3: Democracy will give us what we need.

MARIE: But it *won't*. Look around you. People will just grab for what they can They just want *blood*.

*(Beat.)*

You think these people care about you?

REVOLUTIONARY 3: Sit down.

MARIE: You're nothing to them. You're dispensable. And when they don't need you anymore they'll leave you here to rot.

*(Beat.)*

They won't come for you.
They won't come for you.
You don't have anyone.

REVOLUTIONARY 3 *(A command)*: *Sit down.*

*(Marie sits back down. The Revolutionary cuts. She laughs from the absurdity.)*

MARIE: Well what do I know I'm badly *educated*; what, you think I'm kidding? I'm practically fucking *illiterate* actually. These men of letters? these *Jacobins*? they had more advantages than I ever did: EVER. *(Beat)* Montesquieu Diderot they want you to use *reason*: well guess what? I *can't* reason! I can't do basic *math*! I can't make sense of my *life. Now what?!*

*(He cuts, ignoring her.)*

I was fourteen. I was shipped off to marry a rich French boy who couldn't even tuck his own *shirt* in, I was stripped of *everything.*

*(He won't look at her.)*

*(Despair)* I didn't know what else to *be*
Don't you underSTAND THAT?

*(Pause.)*

REVOLUTIONARY 3: Do you think
   I can *save* you?
MARIE: No.
REVOLUTIONARY 3: Then why are you talking to me.

*(He exits.*
*Time shifts.*
*Marie is alone in her cell.*
*She's aged ten years at least. She's shaking uncontrollably. She's babbling—she's sometimes incoherent.)*

MARIE *(Increasingly unstable)*: November second
   that's when I was born That's my birthday
   All Souls Day Day of the Dead
   but I was bright and shining
   fishermen on the Danube shepherds on the mountains
   bright bright
   then Charles died the smallpox
   *(Beat; then overemphatic)*
   NO JOANNA
   Joanna first then Charles
   Joanna Charles *I can't remember all their names*

[STOP]

Thought I was being protected *how could she protect you* it wasn't rational.
*(Defiant)*
I'm NOT RATIONAL.

*(Beat; quiescent.)*

Brokering marriages she was gone Forging alliances Gone
France gone
Prussia she didn't give a *shit* "QUIET MARIE."

*(Beat; she weeps; she stops; slaps herself violently; points as if speaking to someone else:)*

"an archduchess does *not* shed tears in public."
*(Whispers to herself)*
"Ja Mutter ich werde mich um meine Aufgaben kümmern."

[STOP]

*(We hear the waters of the Seine. She grabs her head in agony.)*

(The sounds are driving me crazy) STOP IT.
(I can't be in a cage) Oh god—I . . . I *can't*—be in a *cage* . . .

*(There's an imperceptible shift in the room. Fersen appears. It should be dreamlike, ethereal.)*

FERSEN: Hello Marie.

*(Marie looks up at him, disbelieving.)*

MARIE: Fersen?

*(She goes to him, tentative at first.)*

I thought they killed you.
FERSEN: No. I'm here.
MARIE: How'd you get in here?
FERSEN: Connections I'm Swedish.

*(She laughs, deep sadness, hugs him, holds him for dear life.)*

MARIE: Oh this is a dream.

*(After a moment, she pulls away.)*

Fersen, we're not royal anymore: they killed Louis, and they took my kids from me, and they won't tell me what's happening.

FERSEN: Don't cry Marie.

MARIE: Sorry You're right, I mustn't forget my deportment.

*(She wipes her eyes hurriedly, assays her old charm.)*

I'd offer you a seat but I've only got this ratty straw mattress which you're welcome to if you don't mind lice.

*(She laughs.)*

FERSEN *(Smiling)*: You look well.

MARIE: *Please*, I look terrible I *smell* terrible.
Look: these inguinal stains, my armpits, I can't stand my own stench. Actually you get used to it, the smells? piss shit they cancel themselves out; the senses putrefy—I'm just faking all this,

FERSEN: What?

MARIE: Hauteur? (I don't know) I have to hold on to *something*.

FERSEN: I don't blame you.

MARIE: You're the only one who doesn't.

FERSEN: You still have adherents.

MARIE: They have made me into something disgusting,
with their pamphlets their smears—

*(Beat.)*

I wish they'd
kill me already //

FERSEN *(Pity)*: Don't say that,

MARIE: Oh do let me be impious *please*.

*(Beat.)*

There's been a trial;
I'm sure to be found guilty.

FERSEN: Of what.

MARIE: Believe me they'll come up with something. They're nothing if not industrious.

FERSEN: What does your lawyer say?

MARIE (*Frayed amusement*): Oh him? he was arrested for treason.

FERSEN: What?

MARIE: Yes I asked if he was tired and they thought we were getting *chummy*.

FERSEN: Oh no.

[STOP]

MARIE (*Sudden drop*): It's no use They want to saw me in half Like a tree Count the ringed interiors So I'll
give it to them.

FERSEN: Don't give up.

(*She's in a mental fog for a moment, then snaps out of it.*)

MARIE: No
(*Trying to cultivate "hope"*)
No of *course* not, I'm very resolute!

(*Beat; then excited—but hypermetabolic.*)

The Austrian army has crossed the border of France, did you know that, a while back? They'll come for me, don't you think? They *have* to. I just have to be patient and they'll come for me. They're my own *people* They'll come for me.

(*Beat.*)

OH: Look!

*(She produces something; hands it to Fersen.)*

FERSEN: What's that.
MARIE *(Covers mouth, giggling)*: One of Louis' watch springs //
FERSEN: No!
MARIE: YES!

*(Laughter.)*

I hid it. I forgot I had it, look it's all rusty //
FERSEN: Louis and his clocks.
MARIE: Yes.

*(Pause.)*

FERSEN *(Sad smile)*: He was wrong you know . . .
MARIE: About?
FERSEN: We should never have called the troops that day.
MARIE: Why not?
FERSEN: The assembly wanted equality, he could have given
    them that.
MARIE: So you believe in this?
    this . . . *democracy*?
FERSEN: Of course not. The surface equality of a single class
    of people makes the exercise of power that much easier;
    it's just a diversion.
MARIE: A diversion?
FERSEN: Power can't be shared that's not the nature of it.
MARIE: No it's like an ether . . .
FERSEN: No such thing as equality . . .

*(Beat.)*

MARIE: Liberty . . .
FERSEN *(Nods no)*: It's an illusion . . .

[STOP]

MARIE *(The question that's been haunting her)*: Has has my life
been a *diversion?*

*(Pause.)*

FERSEN: Don't get eaten up by regrets
     Not now.
MARIE: Should I have married you? or gone away with you?
FERSEN: You couldn't.
MARIE *(Something primal and vulnerable)*: But you *cared* for me.

*(Beat.)*

Maybe these kings and queens and frilly things aren't for me.

*(Beat.)*

I don't know anymore.
It's like some awful dream
and it's never been mine.
FERSEN: What.
MARIE: My life.
FERSEN: Then wake up.

*(Fersen transforms into the Executioner; over the following he
mimes tying Marie's hands behind her back, the ritual of execu-
tion; she's oblivious.)*

MARIE *(Faraway)*: How will you see me a hundred years from
now?

FERSEN: A butterfly with opalescent wings.
MARIE: You're my only friend.

*(Marie is now on the guillotine plank.)*

Fersen. Do you know
I dreamed they pushed me on the guillotine plank
I did and I felt it
I felt my head tighten in the vise
I thought they'd crush it;
*(Small laugh)*
And I had an itch behind my neck but couldn't scratch it
how dumb.
FERSEN/EXECUTIONER: It's not a dream it's real
Wake up to it.
MARIE *(Oblivious)*: They hacked off my head
held it high to thunderous cheers
stuffed it between my dead legs
dumped my body on the grass somewhere
threw it in an unmarked grave . . .

*(Drumroll, shouts.)*

FERSEN/EXECUTIONER: Wake up.
MARIE: But then I became the stuff of history,
And they couldn't kill me

*(She smiles sadly.)*

And when I awoke I thought:
"I have come into life now
Forever."

*(The shouts get louder, more feral. The lights grow blindingly bright. Snap to black.)*